Artist BIOGRAPHIES

Andy Warhol

The Life of an Artist

Carin T. Ford

Enslow Publishers, Inc.

40 Industrial Road	PO Box 38
Box 398	Aldershot
Berkeley Heights, NJ 07922	Hants GU12 6BP
USA	UK

http://www.enslow.com

11/03
JB
Warhol
F

Andy Warhol

Library of Congress Cataloging-in-Publication Data

Ford, Carin T.
   Andy Warhol : the life of an artist / Carin T. Ford.
     p. cm. — (Artist biographies)
   Includes index.
   Summary: Explores the life and career of the twentieth-century American artist,
focusing on his famous works of pop art and many other creative endeavors.
   ISBN 0-7660-1880-6
   1. Warhol, Andy, 1928-   —Juvenile literature. 2. Artists—United States—
Biography—Juvenile literature.   [1. Warhol, Andy, 1928- . 2. Artists. 3. Pop art.]
I. Title. II. Series: Artist biographies (Berkeley Heights, N.J.)
  N6537.W28F674 2002
  700'.92—dc21
  [B]

                           2002011983

Printed in the United States of America

10 9 8 7 6 5 4 3 2 1

To Our Readers: We have done our best to make sure all Internet addresses in this book were active and
appropriate when we went to press. However, the author and the publisher have no control over and assume
no liability for the material available on those Internet sites or on other Web sites they may link to. Any
comments or suggestions can be sent by e-mail to comments@enslow.com or to the address on the back cover.

Illustration Credits: © The Andy Warhol Foundation for the Visual Arts/ARS, NY, © The Andy Warhol
Foundation, Inc.,/Art Resource, NY, pp. 15, 18, 21, 27; © The Andy Warhol Foundation for the Visual Arts/ARS,
NY, © The Andy Warhol Foundation, Inc.,/Art Resource, NY. Andy Warhol Museum, Pittsburgh, Pennsylvania,
U.S.A., p. 25; AP/Wide World Photos, p. 36, 43; Hulton/Archive Photos, pp. 33, 34; Library of Congress, pp. 7,
39; Modern Dance Club from the 1949 Carnegie Tech Yearbook, image used courtesy of Carnegie Mellon
University Archives, p. 11.

Cover Illustration: AP/Wide World Photos

Contents

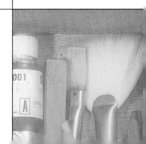

Chapter 1

Early Drawings

Andy Warhola did not like school. He knew it on the very first day.

A girl hit him at school and Andy cried. He told his mother he did not want to go back. He was only four years old. His brother Paul had made him go to school. Paul was the head of the family whenever Andy's father had to travel.

Andy's mother decided to keep Andy home. She enjoyed drawing. For the next two years, Andy and his mother spent many hours together drawing pictures.

Andy would draw and paint pictures for the rest of his life. He liked painting pictures of things people saw every day, in their homes and on supermarket shelves. His paintings included dollar bills, Coca-Cola bottles, and Campbell's soup cans.

This kind of art is called Pop Art. It was very different from any kind of art people had seen before. It was familiar; people could easily understand it. For this reason, Pop Art established itself more quickly than any other movement in art history.

Still, many people were confused by Andy's work. Some called him a genius…others called him a joke.

But Andy—who dropped the final *a* from his last name to make it Warhol—soon became one of the most famous artists in the world. He was known as the Prince of Pop.

The facts about Andy's life are uncertain, and that is the way he liked it.

Andy's childhood in Pittsburgh, Pennsylvania, was not an easy one. His father died when he was fourteen. Andy himself had a number of health problems.

"I never give my background," he once said, "and anyway, I make it all up differently every time I'm asked."

Some facts are known. He was born on August 6, 1928, in Pittsburgh, Pennsylvania. He had two older brothers: Paul, born in 1922, and John, born in 1925.

Andy's parents, Julia and Andrei Warhola, were immigrants. They had left Czechoslovakia in search of a better life in the United States.

When Andy was six, he went back to school. He was a quiet and pale child. He looked sickly. Andy would do his homework after school. Then, he would spend the rest of the afternoon drawing pictures.

Andy became sick with an illness called Saint Vitus' dance when he was eight. The illness made his arms, legs, and face shake. He could not write, speak clearly, or even tie his shoes.

Again, he was kept home with his mother. Julia Warhola bought him comic books, movie magazines, and coloring books. Whenever Andy finished a page in his coloring book, Julia gave him a candy bar. Eventually, he got well.

Andy grew to like drawing portraits of his neighbors and cousins. Soon, he was taking free art classes at Pittsburgh's Carnegie Museum of Art. One of his teachers said, "A more talented person than Andy Warhol I never knew."

Chapter 2

College Years

It seemed as if Andy was drawing all the time. Often, his mother had to bring his dinner up to his room because Andy was too busy drawing to come down for meals.

Shortly before Andy entered high school, his father died. Andrei Warhola had come down with hepatitis, a disease that harms the liver. He had hoped that Andy would be well educated. To make sure of that, he had put some money aside.

At Schenley High School, Andy continued to draw. He carried his sketchbook with him everywhere.

When Andy was close to graduating from high school, he was accepted at both the Carnegie

Modern Dance Club from the 1949 Carnegie Institute of Technology Yearbook. Warhol is seated on the far left.

Institute of Technology and the University of Pittsburgh. The money Andrei Warhola had set aside would pay for his son's college tuition. Andy chose Carnegie because it had the better art department.

He attracted attention as soon as he entered college. The teachers in the art department could not decide whether Warhol was wonderfully talented or had no ability to draw at all. This question is still asked today. That is the mystery of Andy Warhol: Was he a genius or did he just fool people into thinking he was? "If anyone had asked me at the time who was the least likely to succeed, I would have said Andy Warhola," said Robert Lepper, an art teacher at the college.

Warhol was extremely quiet; he almost never spoke. He walked around the campus in baggy blue jeans, a ragged shirt, and torn sneakers.

Often, his art projects had nothing to do with what the teacher had assigned. Sometimes, he handed in ripped pieces of construction paper held together with tape. He even turned in papers that were covered with paw prints from his cat.

By the end of Warhol's first year of college, he was told he must repeat a class he had failed. He also needed to turn in several art projects by the end of summer or he would have to leave school.

Warhol worked hard that summer. He sold fruits and vegetables from his brother Paul's truck every day. While he worked, Warhol drew the people he saw: mothers holding babies, women in ragged clothing.

The sketches were so good that they were displayed in the school. Warhol even won a prize of forty dollars (about three hundred dollars today). Most important, he was allowed to continue college.

Chapter 3

Career Beginnings

As soon as Warhol finished his final year at Carnegie, he moved to New York City. He wanted to get a job as an artist. So, he stuffed his paintings and drawings into a brown paper bag and headed north in 1949.

He had an interview at *Glamour* magazine with editor Tina Fredericks. She was especially impressed by Warhol's style of drawing. He would draw a picture in ink on a piece of paper. Then, he would press this paper down onto a clean sheet of paper and rub hard. The rubbed drawing had a broken-up, or blotted, look to it because not all of the ink transferred evenly.

à La Recherche
du Shoe Perdu
by andy Warhol

Shoe Poems by ralph Pomeroy

Shoes were one of Warhol's first subjects for paintings. As a commercial artist, he won an award for one of his shoe advertisements.

Fredericks wanted to know if Warhol could draw pictures of practical things, such as clothing and shoes.

"I can draw anything," Warhol said.

He was hired.

Soon, several other magazines gave Warhol work. He also illustrated record album covers, greeting cards, and book jackets.

At that time, most young men trying to get jobs in advertising made sure to dress very nicely. But Warhol wore baggy cotton pants, T-shirts, and sneakers. He carried his work in a brown paper bag. During one visit with a magazine editor, a cockroach crawled out of his bag. The editor felt sorry for Warhol and hired him. His friends nicknamed him Raggedy Andy and Andy Paperbag.

Warhol preferred to work through the night and sleep during the day. This was a habit he would continue throughout his lifetime. It was not just because he enjoyed the quiet of night. He was actually afraid of the dark and preferred staying awake.

The amount of time Warhol spent drawing was hard on his eyes. Soon, he began wearing thick glasses.

All through the 1950s, Warhol worked hard as a commercial artist—someone who draws illustrations that help sell products. His name became well known throughout New York City. He earned a lot of money and won many prizes.

But Warhol wanted more.

He once told a friend he wanted to be as famous as the Queen of England. Warhol knew

Warhol became known throughout the world as the artist who made paintings of Campbell's soup cans.

that commercial artists did not usually become famous. But serious artists could.

So he asked his friend, interior designer Muriel Latow, what he could paint that would make people notice him. She told him to paint things that people saw every day at home and in stores. "Something like a can of Campbell's soup," she said.

Warhol liked the idea. He told his mother, who now lived with him in New York, to go to the supermarket. He wanted her to buy every kind of Campbell's soup.

And when he was surrounded by all thirty-two varieties of soup, Warhol began to paint.

Chapter 4

Pop Art Rules

Warhol experimented as he painted. Sometimes the soup cans were very large; other times they were small. Sometimes one soup can filled the entire canvas; other times one hundred cans were in a single painting.

Warhol's paintings were put on sale at a gallery in Los Angeles, California. People were puzzled and amused by his work. Soon, he became known throughout the world as the artist who painted Campbell's soup cans.

Warhol's paintings went on display at other galleries. There were pictures of dollar bills, Coca-Cola bottles, movie stars (such as Marilyn Monroe), and, of course, the soup cans.

Marilyn Monroe (1967). The Monroe portraits were among Warhol's favorites. Marilyn Monroe was a very famous movie star in the 1950s and early 1960s. Warhol started painting her image after she died in 1962.

By the early 1960s, he was considered one of the country's top Pop artists.

Warhol caught the public's attention not only because of his artwork but also because of who he was. He became famous for the way he dressed and the way he spoke. The public seemed to be forever interested in what Warhol would do next.

Using a process called silk-screening, Warhol began painting pictures of disasters: plane and car crashes, funerals, and suicides. He based his silk-screens on newspaper photographs. Often, he repeated one picture over and over on the same canvas, just as he had with the soup cans. He had surprised people with his soup cans, but he shocked them now with his disaster paintings. Warhol was trying to show that anything will begin to feel less shocking—even a horrible car crash—if you look at it over and over again.

Warhol next decided to try sculpture. He used his silk-screening process on wooden crates. He made hundreds of boxes of Campbell's tomato juice, Kellogg's corn flakes, Del Monte peaches, Mott's apple juice, and Brillo pads.

By this time, Warhol had a huge studio to work in. He named it the Factory. He chose this name because he knew that his system of making art was similar to the way products were made on an assembly line in a factory.

Warhol's Brillo boxes were displayed at a New York gallery in 1964. As always, people were amused and fascinated by his latest creations. But the same question kept turning up about Warhol's work: Was it really art?

Silk-Screening

Warhol decided to produce his artwork using a process called silk-screening. Instead of painting the pictures with a brush, he chose a photograph or drew his own picture. Then he prepared a piece of silk in a special way so that it would re-create this picture. He would stretch the silk tight across his canvas. He then forced paint through the silk screen onto the canvas with a rubber roller. But the paint could go only through some parts of the screen and not others because of the way the screen was prepared. The result was a picture on the canvas.

Warhol would use the same screen over and over to turn out many identical paintings in a very short time. He liked the fact that he never actually touched his brush to the canvas. He liked the idea of removing the artist from his artwork. In this way, Warhol thought he was closing the gap between life and art.

"I want to be a machine," he said.

Flowers (1964). Right after he did a series of death and disaster pictures, Warhol was persuaded to make pictures of flowers. He did 900 flower paintings in the summer of 1964.

Chapter 5

Fame Under Attack

Warhol had become famous throughout the world for his paintings and sculptures. Now, he wanted to try making movies.

Warhol still believed that the artist should be removed from his art to make it more real. So, instead of "making" a movie, he often just turned on his camera and let the film roll. The actors could say or do whatever they liked while the film ran.

Self-Portrait (1964). Warhol painted many self-portraits. In fact, one of his exhibits consisted entirely of his self-portraits. It opened in London in 1986. He was quoted there as saying, "If it wasn't me in the pictures, the exhibition would be great."

Sleep was a six-hour film of a man sleeping. *Eat* was a movie in which a man ate a mushroom for forty-five minutes. These films were both silent. Soon, he added music, talking, and color.

Warhol's artwork usually confused people, and so did his movies. Many people thought the films were a waste of time. Others thought Warhol had come up with something new and exciting. But just like Warhol's paintings—which contained any drips and splashes he made—his movies tried to show what real life was like.

As always, Warhol drew attention wherever he went. He now dressed all in black and wore boots, dark glasses, and a silver wig. Andy was very concerned about his weight and often took diet pills to stay thin. The pills also kept him from sleeping very much. He said that from 1965 until 1967, he slept only two or three hours a night.

Warhol did not speak much. One magazine editor said all she ever heard from him were such comments as, "Gee," "Wow," "Really?" "Oh," "Ah," and "Er."

The Factory also drew attention. Everything in the studio was covered with silver paint or aluminum foil. The floor, the ceiling, the furniture, even the cabinets were silver. Millionaires, artists, and actors liked to hang out there.

While he was making movies, Warhol continued to paint. A friend advised him to stop painting disasters and work on something happier. Warhol took the advice and painted hibiscus flowers. He produced hundreds of these paintings. All of them were sold.

Warhol also opened a discotheque (dance club) in New York. The club, called the Dom, was a huge success. It had lights flashing on the dance floor, while five movie projectors showed Warhol's films in the background. The rock group the Velvet Underground performed, and a huge mirrored ball hung from the ceiling.

"He became famous in every field he entered," said Tina Fredericks of *Glamour* magazine. "Even though most people are not sure exactly what Andy was famous for."

Warhol soon became even more famous.

On June 3, 1968, a thirty-two-year-old writer named Valerie Solanas walked into the Factory. She had appeared in one of Warhol's movies. She pulled a gun out of a brown paper bag and shot Warhol in the chest.

He was rushed to the hospital. Although Warhol was pronounced dead, doctors operated on him for more than five hours. He managed to survive.

Warhol stayed in the hospital for six weeks. He thought the gifts he was given of cakes and candies might be poisoned. He asked his nephews to try the food before he would eat it himself.

Solanas was sentenced to three years in prison. By the end of July, Warhol was able to leave the hospital. "Since I was shot, everything is such a dream to me," he said.

But one thing was not a dream. Since the shooting, the value of Warhol's paintings had skyrocketed. Paintings that once cost a few hundred dollars now cost many thousands.

Chapter 6

Famous *and* Rich

Warhol's fame continued to grow. He was treated like a celebrity wherever he went.

His assistants at the Factory decided this was a good time to have a show of Warhol's work. It would include his various series: the soup cans, Brillo boxes, disaster and flower paintings, and portraits. The show would be held in the United States as well as Europe.

The day after the show opened, in 1971 in Pasadena, California, one of Warhol's paintings was sold at Parke-Bernet, a New York auction

This is Warhol in the 1970s, sitting in front of his screenprint of famous boxers. You might recognize Muhammad Ali (top left).

house, for sixty thousand dollars. No living American artist had ever been paid more at auction for his artwork.

Here Warhol poses with a photograph of himself. Notice that he is dressed exactly the same way as in the photo. Warhol was famous for having fun with images in just this sort of way.

Warhol now spent most of his time painting portraits. One of his most popular subjects was China's Communist leader, Mao Tse-tung. In 1973, Warhol painted two thousand pictures of Mao. The pictures ranged in size from six inches to seventeen feet. Some were done on regular canvas, while others were used as wallpaper rolls.

Warhol decided to start a magazine, called *Interview,* that focused on entertainment and fashion. It set the tone for the celebrity magazines that became popular in the 1980s.

Warhol was very busy dividing his time among painting, making films, and publishing a magazine. He worked every day and made a lot of money. But he was always afraid of being poor. He kept a great deal of money stuffed under his mattress, which was made of straw just for him. Warhol also

Warhol with New York real estate developer Donald Trump in 1983. Both men were famous and very controversial.

disliked carrying credit cards. Instead, he walked around with a brown envelope that had several one hundred dollar bills in it.

Warhol enjoyed spending his money and went shopping every day. He considered shopping part of his work. The treasures in his house were worth millions of dollars.

He had many collections: artwork by Pablo Picasso, rare books, bronze statues of horses and dancers, antique furniture, and cookie jars. But Warhol did not like to show off his treasures. In fact, he kept most of the rooms in his house locked.

"He had a routine," said assistant Jed Johnson. "He'd walk through the house every morning before he left, open the door of each room with a key, peer in, then re-lock it. Then, at night when he came home, he would unlock each door, turn the light on, peer in, lock up, and go to bed."

Chapter 7

Last Days

Although he found time every day to go shopping and take his two dogs, Archie and Amos, for a walk, Warhol spent most of his time working. He hated taking vacations and was never able to relax.

In the mid-1970s, Warhol was invited to dinner at the White House by President Gerald Ford. Warhol was very nervous. He wore a white tie and formal dinner jacket. He put on blue jeans underneath his dress pants because they were itchy. He also dyed one of his eyebrows white and the other black, and wore one of his wigs. Warhol would also meet Jimmy Carter, just before he was elected president.

Warhol was hired by the *New York Times Magazine* to do a portrait for their cover of presidential candidate Jimmy Carter.

Warhol published a book in 1975 about his thoughts on life. *The Philosophy of Andy Warhol (From A to B and Back Again)* was based on tapes of Warhol's telephone conversations. He talked about lots of things, including fame, beauty, and death.

The first major show in many years of Warhol's artwork was held in 1977. Andy had painted the symbol of the Communist party, the hammer and sickle. He used silk-screens as well as a large sponge mop to apply the paint in broad strokes.

Warhol began working on an idea for a television show. It was thirty minutes long and included talks with people who were wealthy and famous. *Andy Warhol's TV* ran for nine years. The show seemed to lead the way for the music videos that became popular in the 1980s.

Warhol continued painting. Fifty of his portraits were put on display at the Whitney Museum in New York City. Many art critics did not like the show. They called it boring. One critic said the paintings were awful. "He's right," commented Warhol.

Warhol came out with another book, *POPism*. In the book, he wrote about his view of popular culture in New York. In 1985, he traveled to California and appeared in an episode of the television show *The Love Boat*. He also filmed a commercial for Diet Pepsi.

He was rich and he was famous. But his nephew George said, "I don't think Uncle Andy was very happy at all, even with all that money and fame."

Warhol traveled to Milan, Italy, in 1987 to attend a show of his version of *The Last Supper*. Italian Renaissance painter Leonardo da Vinci had painted the original masterpiece. Warhol had taken the religious work and redone it in his own style, using advertising logos, such as those of General Electric and Dove soap. Although many people came to the opening, Warhol was not able to enjoy it.

He was in a lot of pain because of an infected gallbladder. When he returned to New York, he was operated on immediately. The surgery went smoothly. But the following morning, February 22, 1987, Warhol died of a heart attack. It is unclear why he had the heart attack and whether it was connected to his medical care.

Starting with his paintings of Campbell's soup cans, Andy Warhol brought Pop Art into people's lives throughout the world. He experimented with sculpture, movies, television, magazines, and music.

Many people consider Andy Warhol the most important American artist of our time. But Warhol once said he only wanted to be remembered as a can of soup.

This shot was taken in New York in 1976. Warhol loved photography. His photographs were displayed in one of the last Warhol exhibits before his death.

Timeline

1928 Born Andy Warhola in Pittsburgh, Pennsylvania, on August 6.

1945 Enters Carnegie Institute of Technology.

1949 Begins work as a commercial artist in New York City.

1952 Has first gallery opening.

1962 Displays paintings of Campbell's soup cans.

1963 Begins making films.

1968 Is shot by Valerie Solanas.

1969 Publishes *Interview* magazine.

1971 Shows work at the Pasadena Museum.

1975 Publishes *The Philosophy of Andy Warhol: From A to B and Back Again*.

1977 First major show of new work in ten years features hammer-and-sickle paintings.

1986 Opens show of self-portraits in London.

1987 Dies of heart attack on February 22 after gallbladder surgery.

Words to Know

commercial art — Artwork that is aimed at selling a product, such as a newspaper illustration that advertises shoes.

discotheque — Nightclub where people dance.

immigrant — Person who moves to another country, usually in search of a better life.

logo — Symbol or drawing that people identify with a product, such as the Nike "swoosh."

masterpiece — Artist's work that is generally considered one of the best of its type.

Pop Art — Style of art in which everyday objects, such as soda bottles and light bulbs, were painted or sculpted.

popular culture — Fashions, books, movies, products, and other things enjoyed by ordinary people.

silk-screening — Process using a specially treated piece of silk stretched across a canvas. It works somewhat like a stencil. An artist can make the same exact design over and over again.

Andy Warhol

Internet Addresses

The best way to learn more about any artist, including Andy Warhol, is to see the art—the real thing, not just photographs of it. That is easy if you happen to live in a large city with a large art museum, such as New York or Pittsburgh. But if you do not, try the Internet. The Web sites for Warhol listed on the next page were written for people of all ages, so the text may be a bit too hard for you to get through. That is okay, though—you are just visiting for the pictures.

The Andy Warhol Museum If you cannot get over to Pittsburgh, Pennsylvania, take a virtual tour of an entire museum devoted to Andy Warhol.

http://www.warhol.org

Artcyclopedia, the Fine Art Search Engine: Andy Warhol This site has links to nearly 70 works by Warhol that can be viewed online, as well as to books and articles about his life.

http://www.artcyclopedia.com/artists/warhol_andy.html

Index

THE AMAZING BOOK OF
CARD TRICKS

A STEP-BY-STEP ILLUSTRATED GUIDE
TO A HOST OF SIMPLE YET SPECTACULAR TRICKS

JON TREMAINE

Bramley
Books

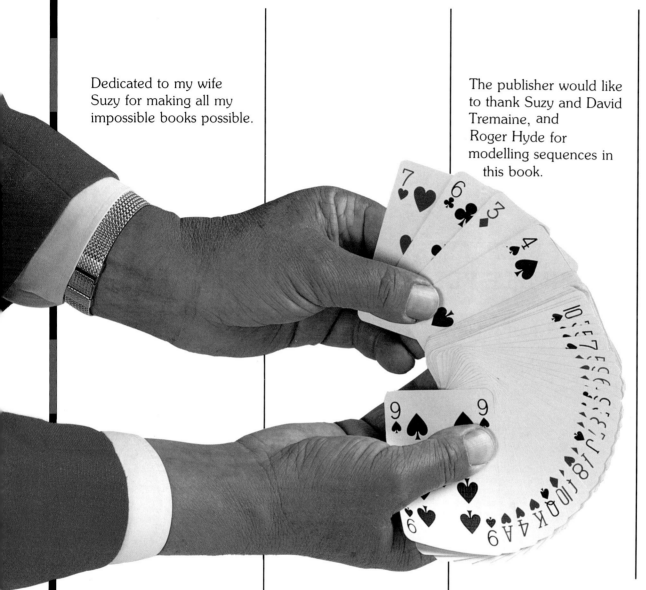

Dedicated to my wife Suzy for making all my impossible books possible.

The publisher would like to thank Suzy and David Tremaine, and Roger Hyde for modelling sequences in this book.

Credits

Photography
Neil Sutherland

Editor
Philip de Ste. Croix

Designer
Stonecastle Graphics Ltd

Production
Ruth Arthur
Sally Connolly
Neil Randles
Karen Staff
Jonathan Tickner

Director of production
Gerald Hughes

Typesetting
SX Composing Ltd, Essex

Colour reproduction
Scantrans PTE Ltd,
Singapore

Printed in Singapore
Star Standard Industries
(Pte) Ltd.

3497 Amazing Book of Card Tricks
This edition published in 1999
by Bramley Books, a division of
Quadrillion Publishing Ltd
Copyright © 1994 Quadrillion
Publishing Ltd, Woolsack Way
Godalming, Surrey GU7 1XW
All rights reserved
ISBN 1-85833-276-1

THE AUTHOR

Jon Tremaine has been a world class professional magician for nearly thirty years. He is a member of London's Inner Magic Circle, and has been honoured by them with a Gold Star, the highest award that a magician can receive. He has appeared on television, and travelled the world entertaining in top night clubs, hotels and cruise liners. His particular speciality is close-up magic, the most difficult branch of magic to perform; its exponents are few, and Jon is undoubtedly one of the very best. He is the author of a set of four books about performing magic specifically for children – the series is entitled "Let's Make Magic". He is married and lives in Cuckfield, Sussex, England.

INTRODUCTION

I am going to show you how to do some outstanding magic tricks. You will learn to do some amazingly simple "sleight-of-hand" movements that will fool your audience completely. Some of the subtleties that you will learn are so cheeky that you will probably say to yourself:

"How on earth will I be able to get away with it without the audience realizing what I am doing?"

Don't worry! Take my word for it. If you are prepared to *practise*, there is no limit to the heights of skill that you will achieve or the degree of bewilderment that you will create by using the methods that I describe.

The secret of performing successful magic is to realize that 90 per cent of the effect of a trick is merely *presentation* or acting. There are even some tricks that are *100 per cent presentation*, requiring no manipulative skill at all! Successful *presentation* will make your tricks *entertaining* and *magical* – not simply novelty puzzles of limited interest to your audience. Your success will be due to a thorough knowledge of the workings of the trick and hours of dedicated practice before showing it to anyone.

I can give you the knowledge. No problem. However, only you can put in the *practice* that will lead you to a successful performance! The more practice you put in, the more you will get out of your magic, and the more your audience will be entertained by it. Secrecy is also important. The motto of The Magic Circle, the most famous and exclusive magic club in the world, is: *Indocilis Privata Loqui* (Not apt to disclose secrets) or, as we members more loosely translate it, "Keep your mouth shut!"

Do not pass your secrets on to others!

Why then am I writing this book and "spilling the beans"?

In buying this book, you have made a commitment. You have shown more than a passing interest in the world of magic and are obviously not just idly curious. If you want to perform tricks, you have got to start somewhere. Nobody is born a magician. Like all other skills, it must be learned.

I started by getting a book out of my local library. I was immediately "hooked". I soon discovered the joy in fooling other people. Four years later I gave up a promising career in architecture to become a magical entertainer. Maybe you will get hooked too!

I know that you will enjoy this book. You will learn a great deal. Just how far you go with this knowledge will be up to you. At best it could be the beginning of an exciting career for you. At the worst it will give you an insight into the fascinating world of magic and teach you a few tricks that you will delight in demonstrating to your friends. Your popularity will increase and so will your confidence.

Go for it!

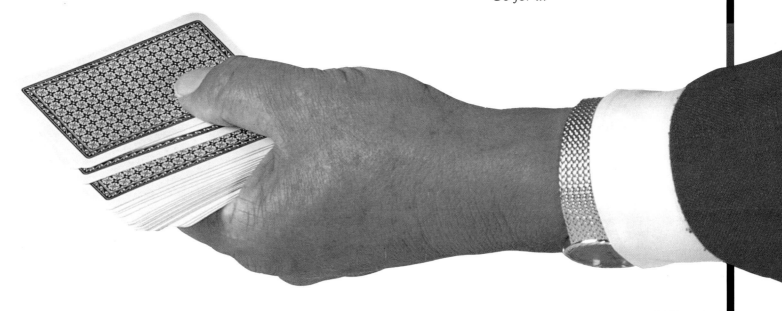

PART ONE

BASIC HANDLING SKILLS

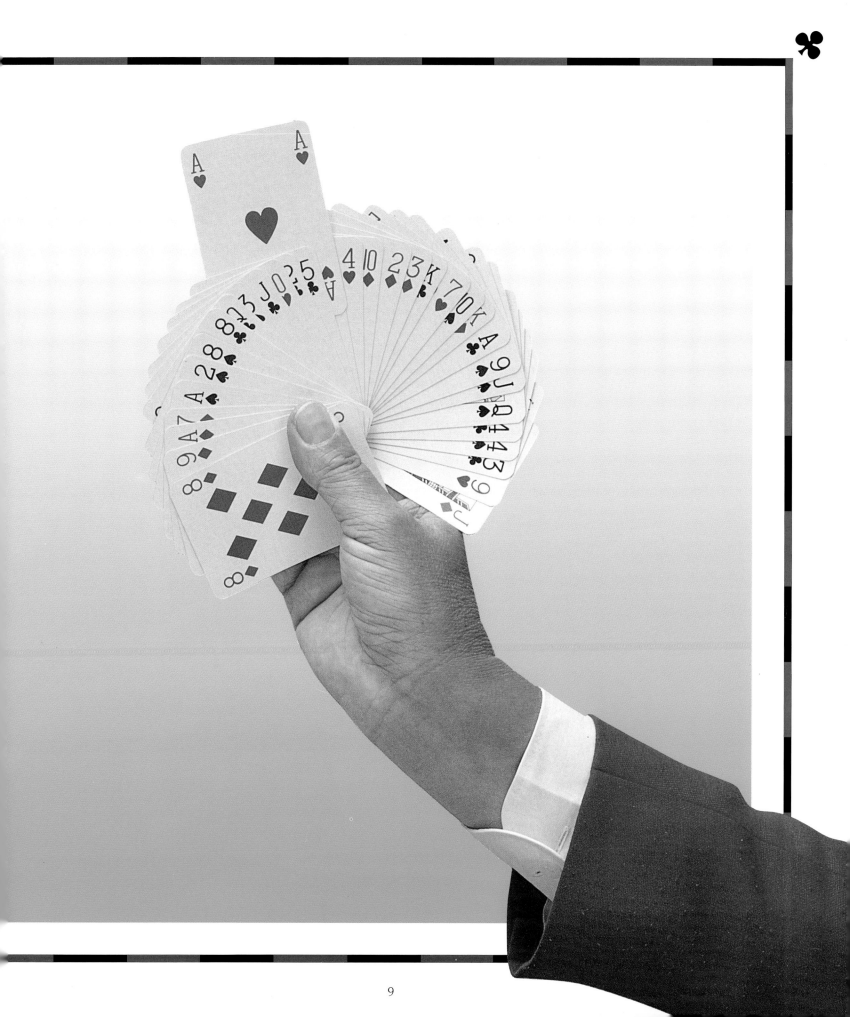

CARD HANDLING

This first section starts by teaching you how to handle a pack of cards and how to perform sleight-of-hand feats and numerous subtleties with them. Then, your efforts in mastering basic handling skills will be rewarded by the disclosure of some two dozen super magical tricks that you will now be able to perform using the knowledge that you have gained from studying this section of the book. So, in no time at all, you will have a whole string of outstanding card tricks up your sleeve!

If you cannot find a pack of cards at home, go out and buy one. On second thoughts, buy three – two with *blue* backs and one with *red* backs. The spare blue pack will be used for making up "special" cards and supplying the odd duplicate card that you may need for certain tricks.

Cards with a linen finish are best, although plastic coated cards are also nice to use. Cards that are just described as plastic are not easy to manipulate, because the material is too hard. It will make life easier, too, if you buy packs with white borders around the back designs. Why? Because occasionally a trick may require a card to be secretly reversed (i.e. turned over) in the pack. The white border of the back design will prevent it from being exposed prematurely.

The cards that we will be using for most of our tricks will have *blue* backs. It is a more positive colour than red and is more easily seen.

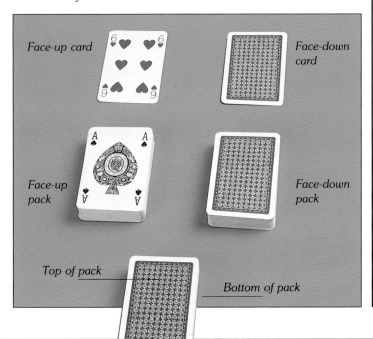

Face-up card

Face-down card

Face-up pack

Face-down pack

Top of pack

Bottom of pack

THE LANGUAGE OF THE CARD MAGICIAN

There are many special words used by card magicians and you will need to remember them so that the explanations in the tricks section make sense.

♣ OVERHAND SHUFFLE ♣

A *shuffle* alters the order of all the cards in the pack. Your right hand grasps some of the cards from the back section of the pack (**1**) (assuming you are right-handed) and lifts them up and over the front part of the pack (**2**). Your left thumb now pulls off a card or bunch of cards (**3**) and keeps doing this until all the cards that were held in the right hand are now deposited on top of the original left hand group (**4**). This action is repeated a few times and a very good mix is thus obtained. Later on I will show you how to *false shuffle* the pack: apparently mixing all the cards up while actually keeping control of any card or cards that you choose to. Like the four Aces!

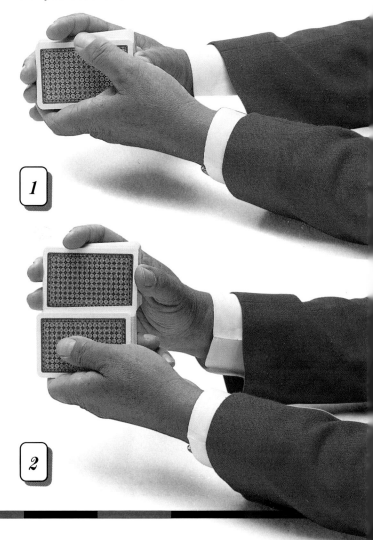

1

2

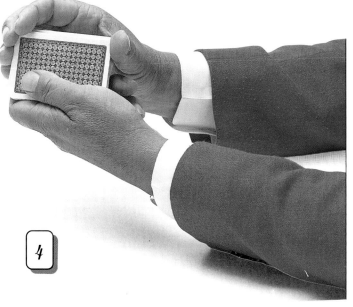

◄ CUTTING ►

To "cut" the pack is to divide the cards by lifting off some of the cards and placing them to the side (**5**). To "complete the cut" is to put the remainder of the pack on top of the cards that you have just lifted off (**6**).

◆ CARD SPREAD ◆

A card spread can be executed across a table (**7**) or between your hands in the action of having a card chosen by a spectator (**8**).

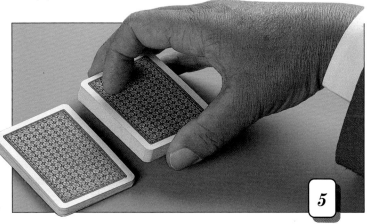

5

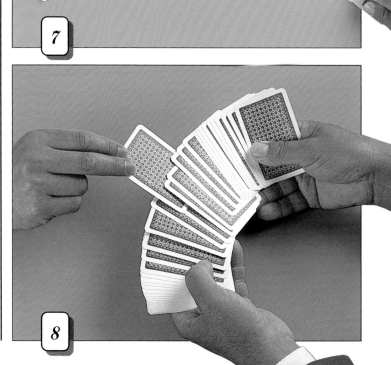

7

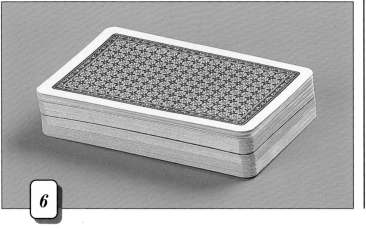

6

8

♥ OVERHAND FALSE SHUFFLE ◀

When you do a *false* overhand shuffle it must *look* exactly like the genuine one that you have already practised. To practise the false shuffle put the four Aces on top of the pack (**1**).

Lift the bottom half of the pack upwards as before (**2**). (This is called *undercutting*). Your left thumb now draws a card off the top of this half so that it lands on top of the four aces. At the same time slide it *inwards* so that it projects about 10mm over the edge (**3**). (This is called an *injog*). Shuffle off the rest of the cards unevenly on top of the *injogged* card so that the fact that it is sticking out a bit is less obvious (**4, 5**).

Your right hand now undercuts the pack again by pushing upwards on the underside of the injogged card (**6, 7**), grasping all the cards below it and throwing them (still in one block) back on top (**8, 9**).

The four Aces are now back on top!

In magicians' language you have just undercut the pack, injogged one card, shuffled off, undercut at the injog and completed the cut! Aren't you clever! With practice, the injog can be very small indeed – just a couple of millimetres – hardly noticeable at all.

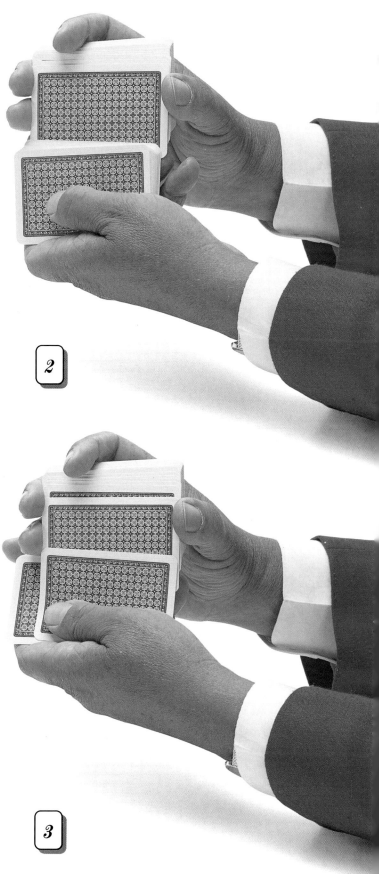

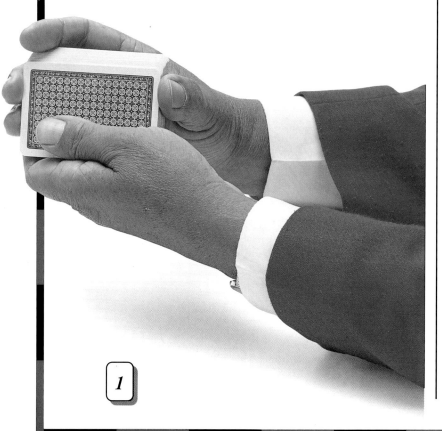

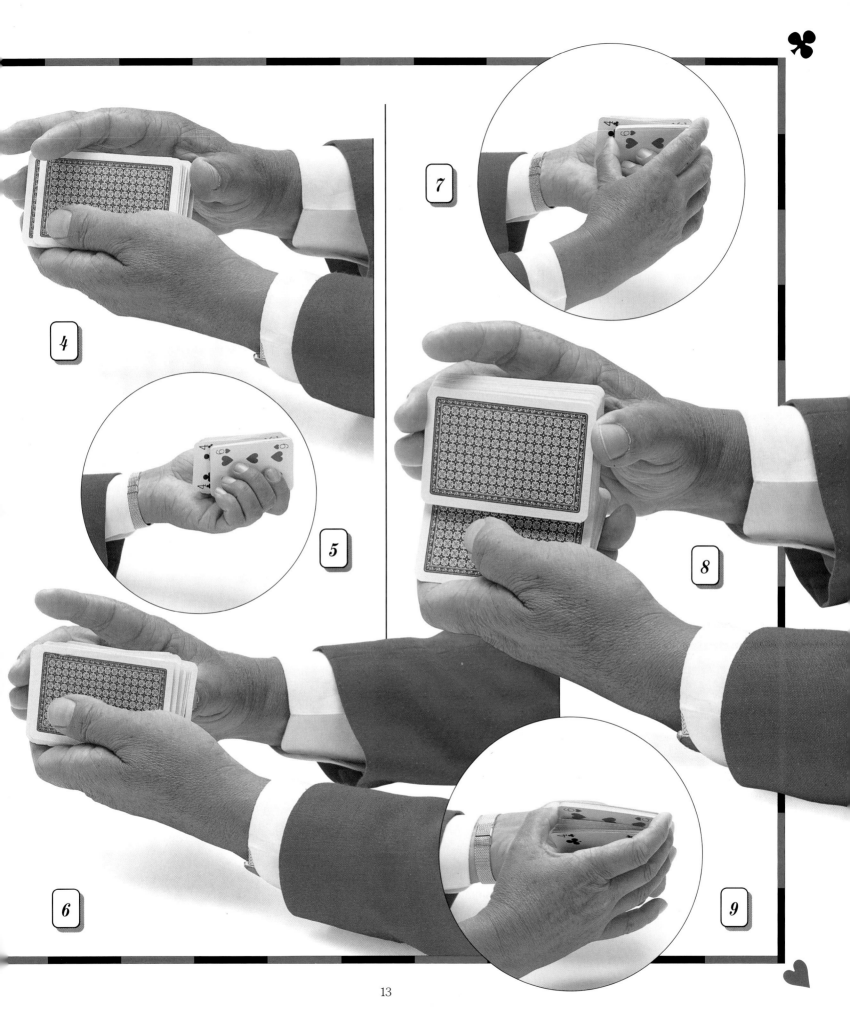

If a trick requires you *to shuffle the top card to the bottom*, proceed as follows:

Hold the complete pack in your right hand in the shuffling position. In this example, the eight of Spades is the top card (**1**). Draw off the top card *only* into your left hand by dragging it there with your left thumb (**2**). Now shuffle off the rest of the cards on top of this card (**3**). The card that was originally on top is now on the bottom (**4**).

To *shuffle the bottom card* (**5**) *to the top*:

Just start a normal shuffle (**6**) by undercutting the bottom half (**7**). Hang on to the original bottom card until last (**8**) and deposit it on top as you complete the shuffle (**9, 10**).

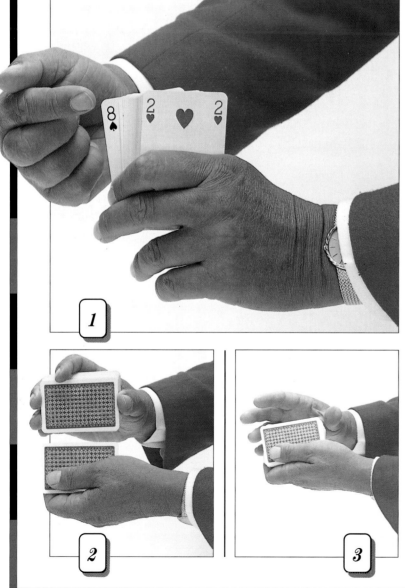

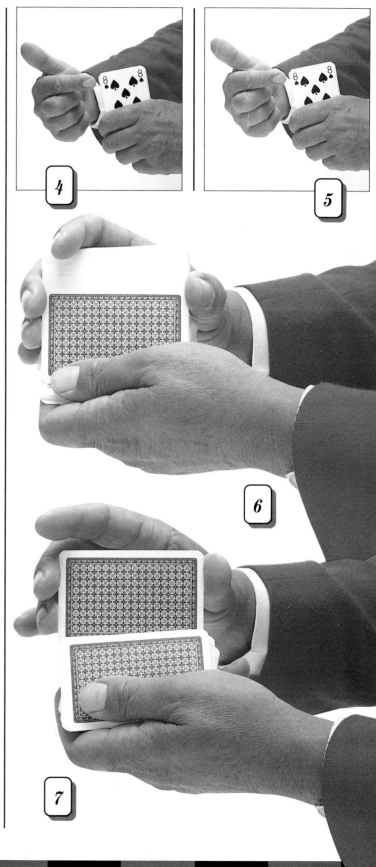

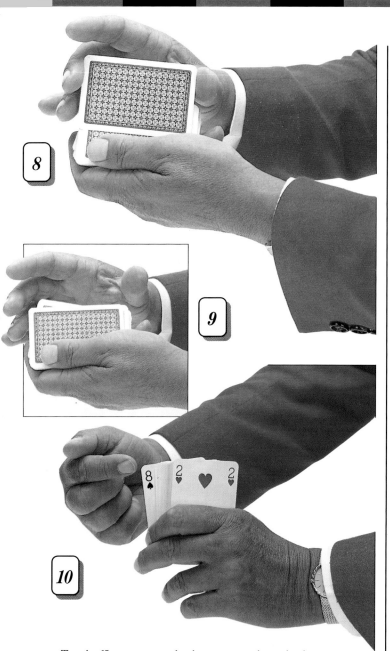

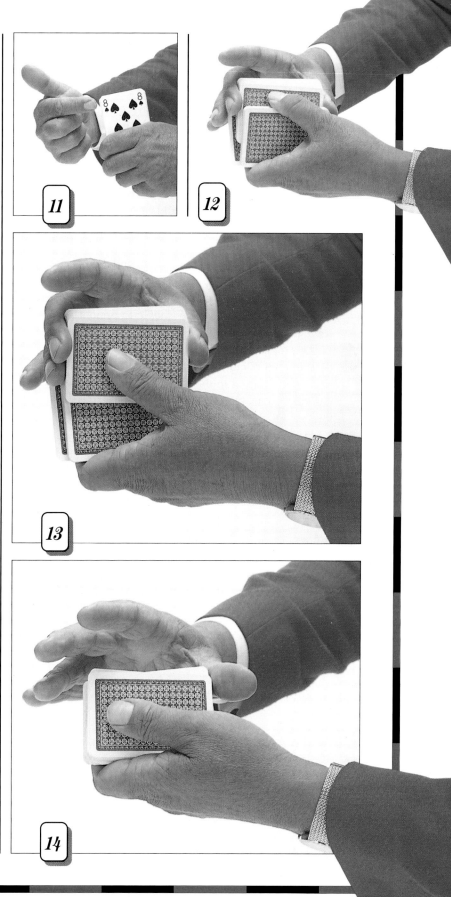

To *shuffle retaining the bottom card on the bottom* (**11**): Let the fingers of your left hand press on the face of the bottom card. As you undercut, let these fingers drag on the bottom card so that it is retained in your left hand (**12**). The original top half of the pack falls on it and the undercut bottom half of the pack in your right hand is now shuffled off in the normal way (**14**).

You are now executing *overhand shuffle control*. You must practise these actions until they become smooth and second nature to you. To avoid drawing attention to them, your shuffles should always appear to be casual. Not sloppy – just a little haphazard and natural looking.

OVERHAND SHUFFLE PRACTICE ROUTINE

This routine will help you practise the various card controls that I have just explained. Perform the complete routine over and over again until it becomes smooth and seamless in execution.

1 To help you keep track of what you are doing turn the top card face up!

2 False shuffle the pack to bring the top card back to the top by undercutting the pack, injogging one card, shuffling off, undercutting at the injog and throwing the block of cards on top. Your reversed card should now be on top again.

3 Shuffle the top card to the bottom and then back to the top again.

4 Shuffle the top card to the bottom. Shuffle again to keep it on the bottom. Now shuffle to bring it to the top again.

The simplest application of the overhand false shuffle is in controlling a spectator's chosen card once it has been returned to the pack. The pack is then apparently shuffled fairly and the chosen card lost forever! Or so the spectator thinks!

1 Shuffle the cards.

2 Spread the cards face downwards between your hands and have the spectator remove the card.

3 Ask him to look at his card and remember it.

4 Undercut the pack and have the spectator replace his card on top of the pile in your left hand.

5 Carry on with the shuffle, injogging the first card, shuffling off, undercutting at the injog and throwing the block on top.

6 The chosen card will now be on top, although the spectator will think that it is lost somewhere in the middle of the pack.

7 You can now deal with his card as the particular trick that you are performing dictates.

♣ PALMING ♣

To palm a card means to hide a card or cards secretly in the palm of your hand. Palming is used when you wish secretly to remove a card (or cards) from the top of the pack. It can also be used secretly to add cards to the top of the pack.

Hold the pack face downwards in your left hand. Let your thumb push the top card forward just a little (**1**), (an *outjog*). Bring the right hand over to the left and let your finger tips gently rest along the protrud-

ing edge (**2**). In this position, the palm of your right hand completely covers the pack.

Now, if you press down with your fingertips, the outjogged card will pivot upwards into your palm (**3**). Arch your hand slightly so that you get a grip on the card using only your palm and finger tips. The card will follow the contours of your arched hand.

Move your right hand slightly to the right until your thumb is able to grip the nearside short end of the pack. You can now hold the complete pack between your thumb and fingers with the card still concealed in your palm (**4**). Move your left hand away. The whole action should look as if you have merely transferred the pack from one hand to the other.

When you first try to palm a card it will feel as if you are trying to conceal a sack of potatoes! Please do not worry about it. Keep practising and it will suddenly all fall into place. Palming is always done on the "off beat" – the right psychological moment – when the spectator is distracted by your patter and least prepared to spot your sleight of hand.

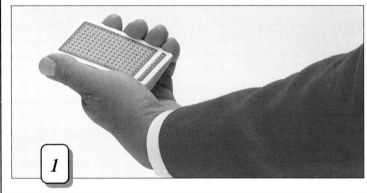

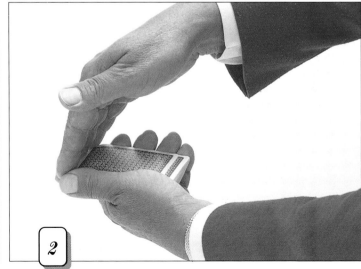

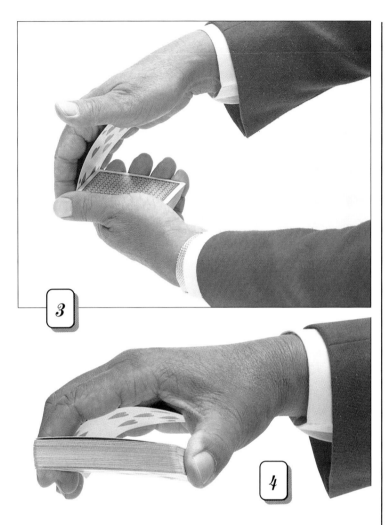

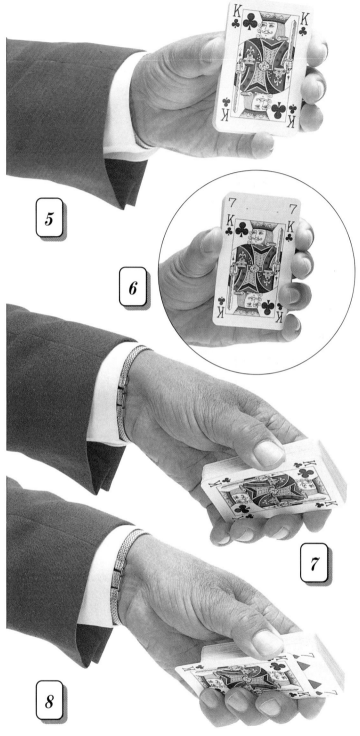

❧ THE GLIDE ❧

This extremely useful dodge enables us to achieve two things. If you show the bottom card of the pack and deal it onto the table, the *glide* enables you to change it for an entirely different one. We can also deal from the bottom of the pack and yet retain the bottom card where it is until we need it! For example, a chosen card can be secretly shuffled to the bottom. You could ask the spectator to call out a number under 20. Supposing he says "nine", if you started dealing cards from the bottom, the ninth one dealt will be his selected card! Very crafty!

Hold the pack, as shown, with your thumb on one long edge and your fingers curled under the other edge. Twist your wrist to show the bottom card (**5**). In our example, it is the King of Clubs which has the seven of Diamonds directly beneath it (**6**). Now return the pack to a face downward position by twisting your

wrist the opposite way. As you do this, you pull back the bottom card with your left second and third finger tips (**7, 8**). This *small* action is disguised by the *larger* action of turning the hand over. By *gliding* back the bottom card in this way, you have exposed about a centimetre of the second from bottom card.

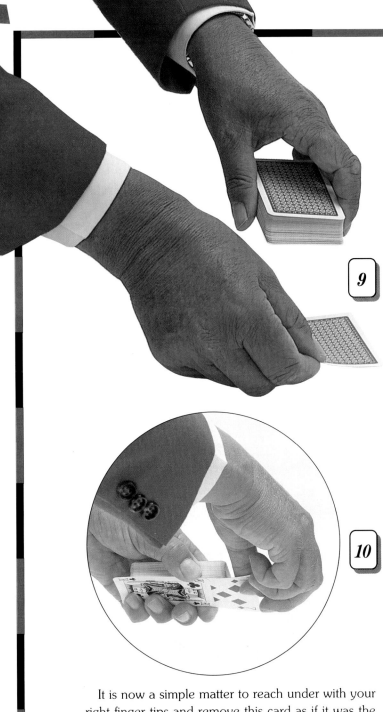

Secretly get a little finger break under the top two cards (**1**). Push both cards forward about 2cm with your right thumb (**2**). Grasp the two cards at the protruding end (**3**). Turn them both over and place them face upwards on top of the pack, still protruding a little (**4**). Be careful to keep the two cards exactly aligned so that they appear "as one" at all times. Now repeat the action, turning them face down again and this time squaring them up with the rest of the pack.

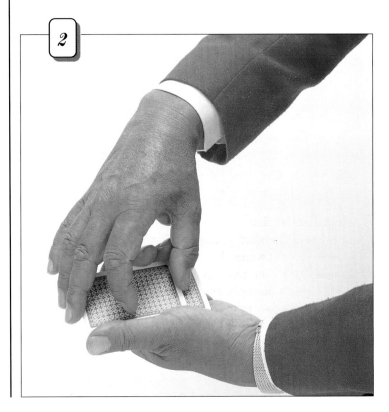

It is now a simple matter to reach under with your right finger tips and remove this card as if it was the bottom one and deal it upon the table (**9, 10**). You can now slide the bottom card back flush with the rest of the pack, and nobody will be any the wiser.

◆ THE DOUBLE LIFT ◆

The sleight we call a *double lift* is extremely useful. In simple terms it is the act of picking up *two* cards from the top of the pack and showing them as if you were only holding *one*. This way you can show that the real top card is not the top card at all!

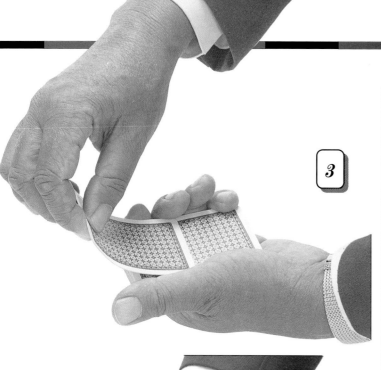

cards aligned. To complete the sequence, just reverse the movements and replace the "double lift" back on the top of the pack.

Simple Use

Control a spectator's card to second from top of the pack. Double lift to show that it is apparently the top card. Replace double lift. Remove the real top card and, without showing its face, bury it in the centre of the pack. Make a "magic pass" and show that the chosen card has magically jumped back to the top of the pack again!

Practise the double lift until you can perform it smoothly and effortlessly. It is a valuable weapon and you will be asked to use it often.

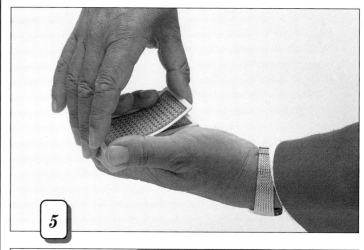

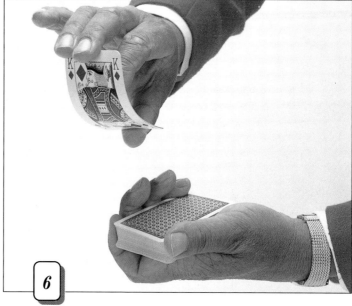

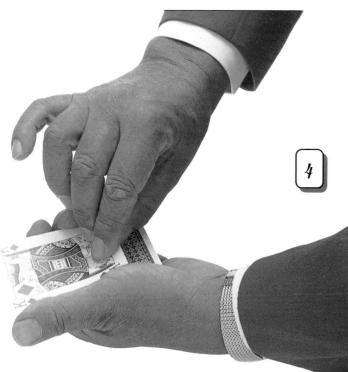

Lift Number Two

You may need to "double lift" without turning the cards face upwards. In this case, you secure a finger break under the top two cards as before. Now reach over with your right hand. Place your thumb at the nearside edge, your third and fourth fingers on the opposite edge (**5**) and your index finger pressing lightly on the centre of the top card.

Lift the top two cards up (as one) and show the visible face to the spectator (**6**). Notice how the cards are *slightly* curved. This curvature helps keep the two

FORCING

For certain effects it is necessary to force the spectator to choose a specific card while apparently letting him have a completely free choice! Without this ability, the desired effects cannot be achieved. I will now teach you a few ways to do this. Practise them all and use the method with which you feel most comfortable.

The following forces all start with the card to be forced on top.

➤ FORCE 1: X-ING THE PACK ➤

False shuffle the pack and then ask the spectator to cut the pack in half (**1, 2**). Pick up the *bottom* half and rest it across the top half, like this (**3, 4**). Now you distract his attention by talking!

"You could have cut the cards anywhere, couldn't you?"

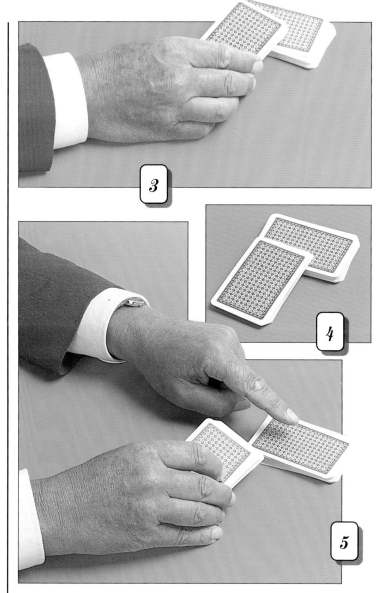

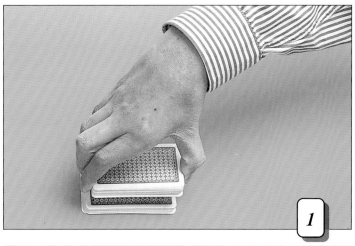

Point to the cards and say:

"And we have marked where you cut like this . . ."

Lift off the half that is resting on top and point to the top card of the half that remains on the table (**5**).

"Look at the card that you cut to, and remember it."

Of course it is your force card, the one that was originally the top one. When you talk to the spectator, it has the effect of distracting him. He will be unable to recall the exact sequence of events and will never question your bare-faced cheek!

♣ FORCE 2: SLIP CUT FORCE ♣

This is a simple yet very convincing force. Here, we shall use the nine of Hearts (**6**). False shuffle the pack and then hold it in your left hand as shown.

Your left thumb now riffles the pack at its upper left corner (**7**) and the spectator is invited to say *Stop* whenever he wishes. When he says "Stop", you stop riffling immediately and hold the gap. Your right hand now approaches your left and grasps the cards above this break between the thumb at the inner end and the second, third and fourth fingers at the outer end (**8**).

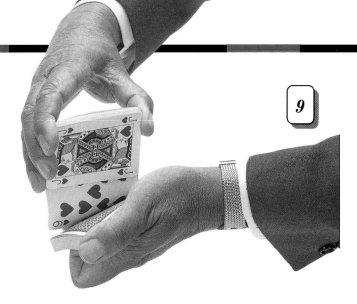

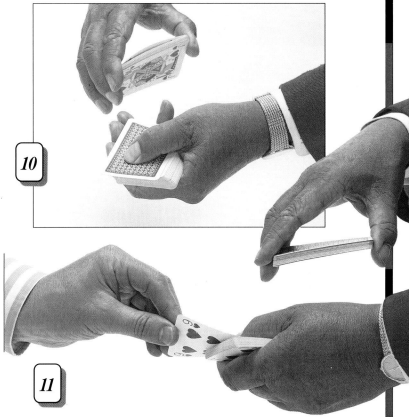

The second, third and fourth fingers of your *left* hand now press firmly on the top card, dragging it back and preventing it being lifted away with the rest of the cards by the right hand (**9**). This action secretly transfers the force card from the top of the whole pack to the top of the lower half which was created when the spectator called "Stop"! Your left hand now extends the lower half of the pack to the spectator (**10**) as you say:

"Please take the card that you cut to (11)."

◆ FORCE 3: HANKY PANKY FORCE ◆

You will need a good quality handkerchief or napkin to perform this highly effective force. False shuffle keeping the card to be forced (the ten of Clubs in this instance, **1**) on the top. Place the pack face downwards on your right palm (**2**). Cover your hand and the cards with the handkerchief (**3**). *As you cover your hand, flip the pack over so that it is now face up (**4**)!* Practise until you can do it smoothly.

Ask the spectator to cut the pack *through* the handkerchief (**5**). As soon as he lifts his cards high enough, secretly flip the cards in your hand face down again (**6, 7, 8**) while still under cover of the handkerchief. Offer your right hand with your cards resting on the palm (**9**) and say,

"Take the card that you cut to."

Finally take away the handkerchief containing the other cards with your free hand. Simple but very effective! He has taken the ten of Clubs!

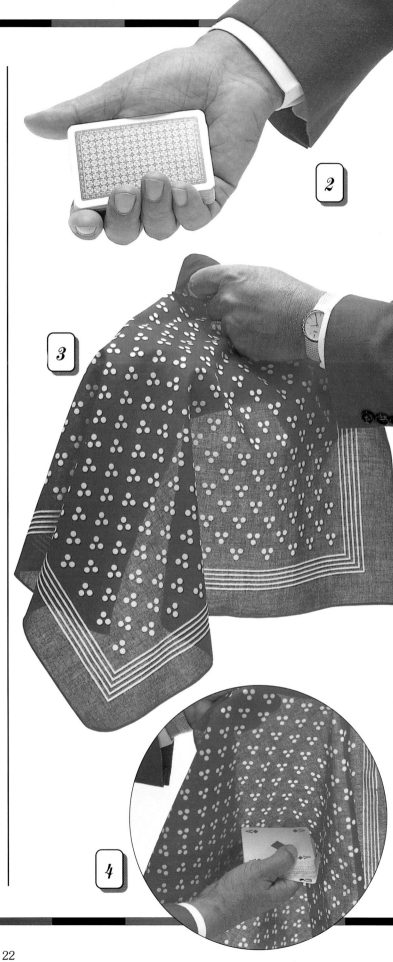

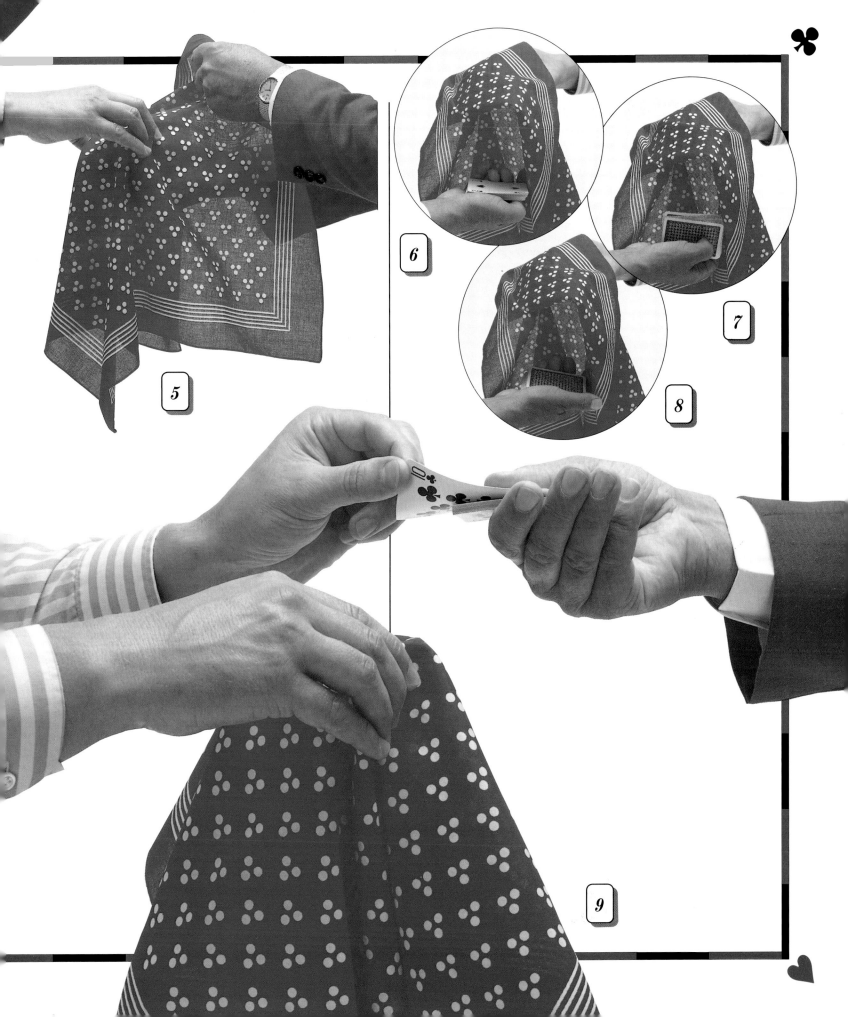

5

6

7

8

9

❥ FORCE 4: CROSS HAND FORCE ◀

False shuffle the cards. Hold the pack in your left hand.

"I am going to do this trick without looking at the cards."

Put the cards behind your back (**1**). As soon as they are out of sight, slip the card to be forced off the top and slide it over into the palm of your right hand (**2, 3**) and cover it over with your left hand (**4**). Turn around so that your back is now facing the spectator.

"Now, I want you to take the pack (5). Give the cards a very good shuffle (6), then put them back on my hand again (7)."

As soon as you get the pack back, turn around to face the audience and secretly slide the concealed card back on top of the pack again (**8, 9**). With a little practice you should be able to do this without anyone noticing your arms move.

"Did you really give them a good shuffle?"

"Yes" says the spectator. Turn your back on her again (**10**).

"Right, take off the card that you have shuffled to the top . . ."

She does so (**11**) and you have successfully forced the top card (**12**)!

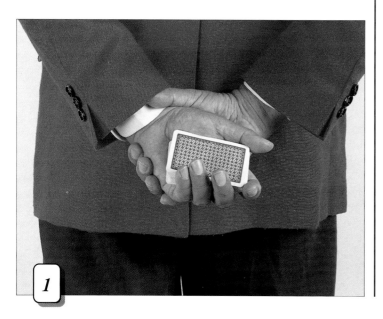

24

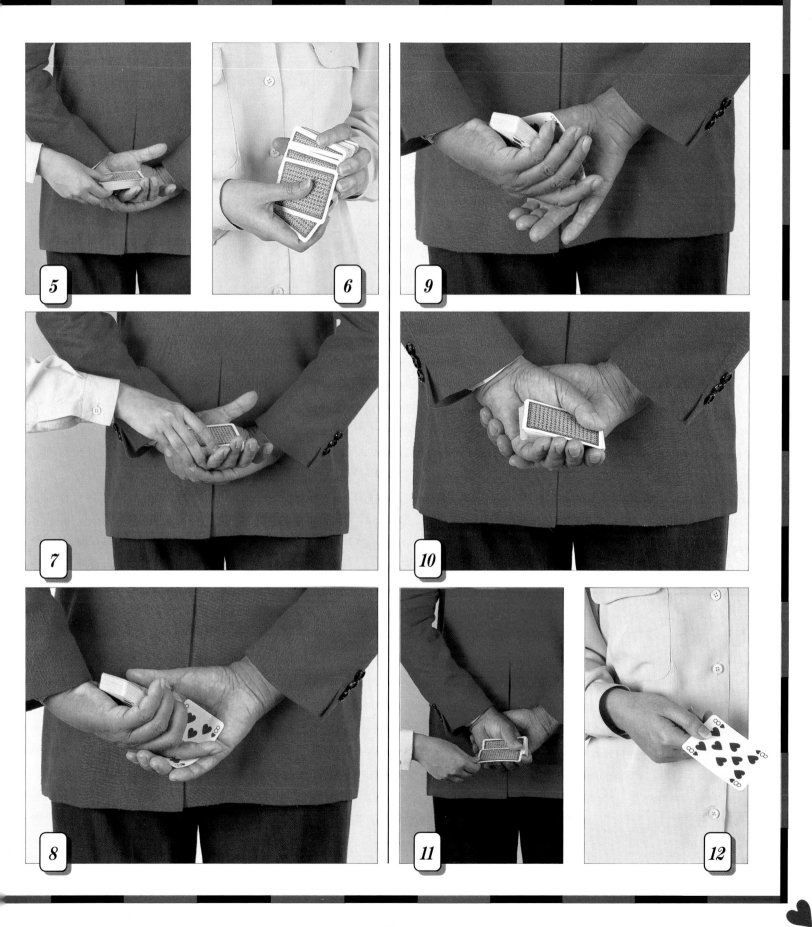

SELECTED CARD TRICKS

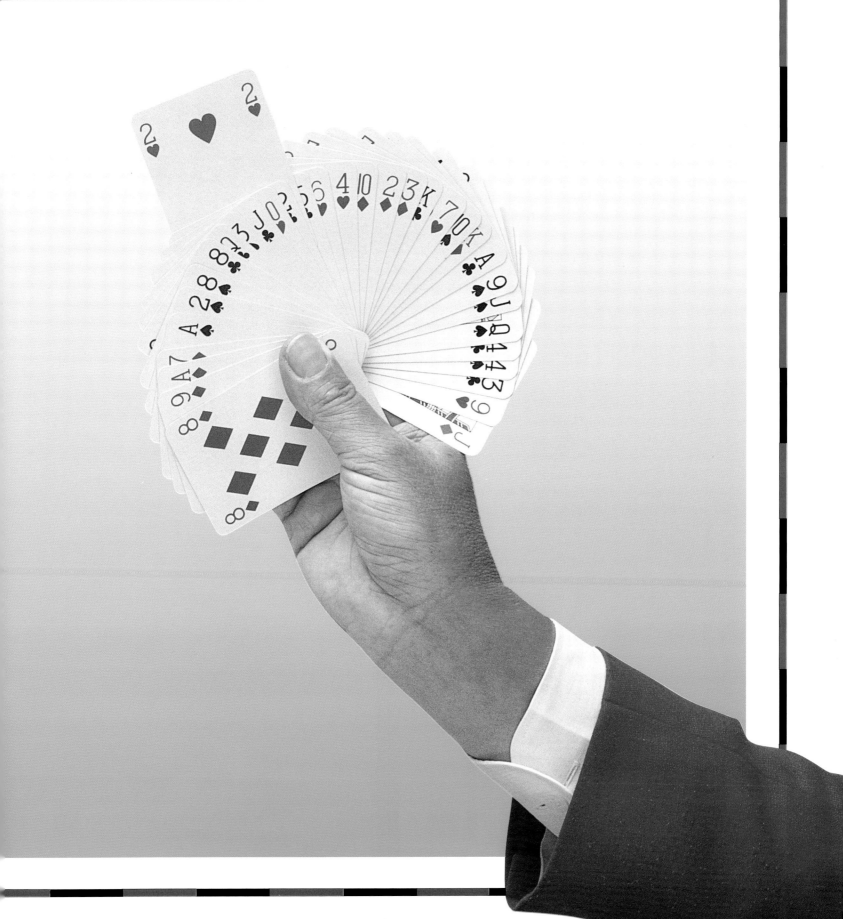

ACROBATIC ACES

I will start you off with a favourite theme among card magicians. Four Ace tricks always create interest – especially among card players!

♣ EFFECT ♣

The four Aces demonstrate their acrobatic ability by disappearing from the pack and appearing in a spectator's pocket!

◀ WHAT YOU DO ▶

Remove the four Aces and lay them face upwards on the table (**1**). Hold the rest of the pack face downwards in your left hand. Ask a member of the audience to tell you which Ace is his favourite. As I am sure he has never been asked that question before it should take him a couple of seconds for the question to sink in and for him to make his choice.

While he is making up his mind, secretly lift up the edge of the top *three* cards and insert the tip of your little finger in the gap, holding a break (**2**). When he has chosen his Ace (say the Ace of Hearts), pick it up and place it *face up* on top of the pack (**3**). Place the other three Aces on top of it (also face up) (**4, 5**). Then, with your right hand, pick up the Aces, together with the three cards above your finger break *as one block* (**6**).

You now have to show these *seven* cards as if they are only *four*! This is how you do it.

At the moment you are holding a block of seven cards in your right hand, (three face-down indifferent cards covered by the four face-up Aces). Hold these over the pack, covering about half of it. Do not let go of your grip. Drop your left thumb on the top Ace and press lightly.

REQUIREMENTS
Just a pack of cards and a spectator

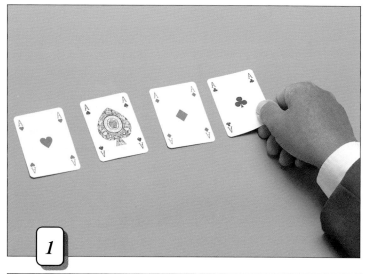

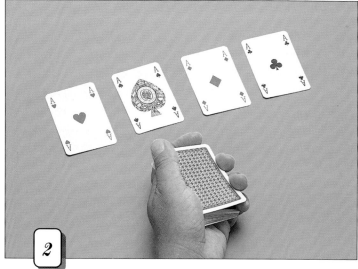

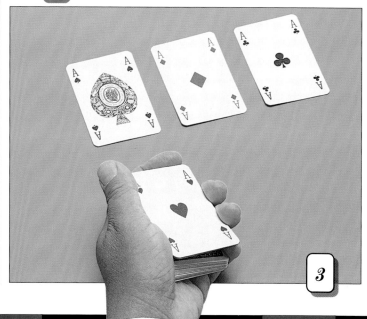

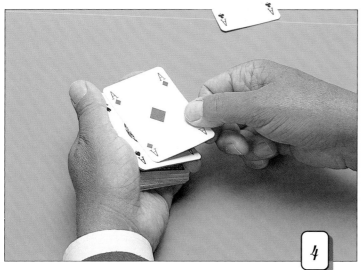

Move your right hand and the remaining (six) cards away to the right again (**7**). The left thumb's pressure prevents the top Ace from moving with them. It stays put. Just before the six cards clear the right hand edge, you use them to flip this Ace over so that it ends up face down on top of the pack (**8, 9**). These three actions should be practised until they blend into one smooth movement – the act of just flipping a card over.

Repeat the action with the next Ace making sure that you keep the cards aligned so that the extra three are not revealed in any way. Now flip the third Ace over. This leaves you with the chosen Ace face up (**10**). Hidden beneath it, unknown to the spectator, are the three odd cards. Drop the whole pile on top of the pack (**11**) and then instantly flip the last Ace face downwards (**12, 13**). This *looks* exactly like the movement you have performed three times already – only this time you have secretly placed three odd cards under the top Ace.

In order from the top should now be the chosen Ace, then the three odd cards, and then the other three Aces (**14**). From your point of view you have just completed the technical 10 per cent of the trick. The dirty work has been done! Now comes the *presentation* – the other 90 per cent – which will turn this into a great trick. Deal the top four cards face down in a row from left to right (**15, 16**).

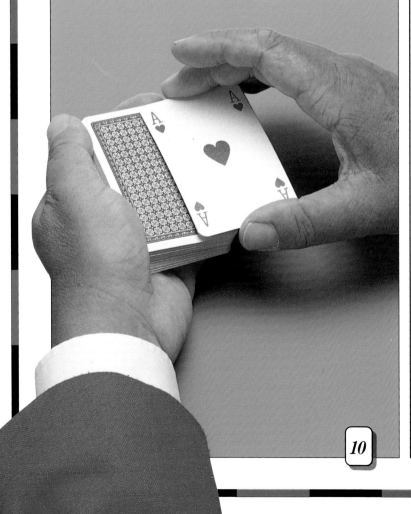

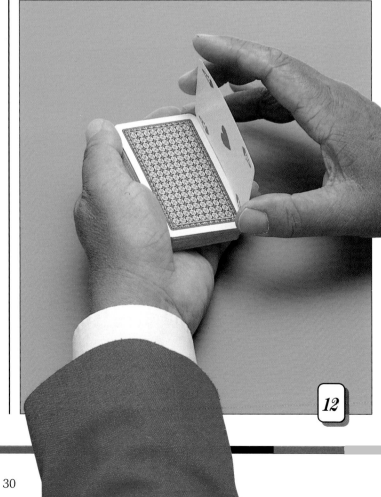

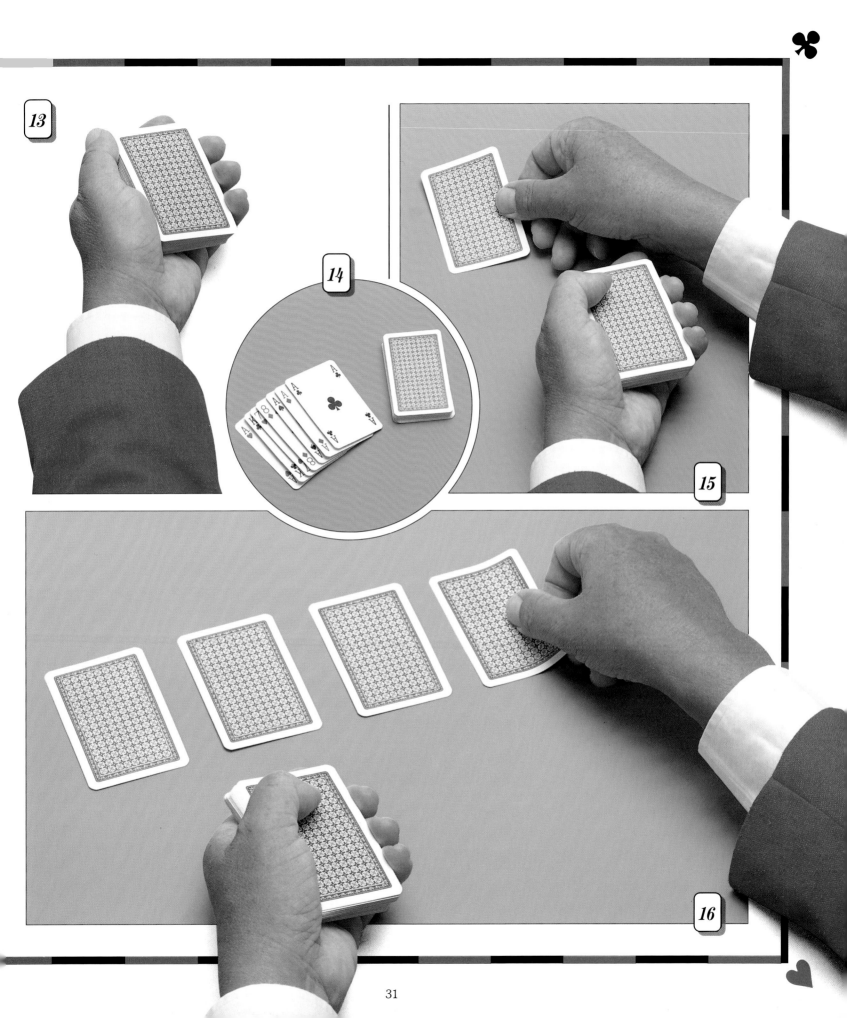

"I'll just deal the Aces onto the table."

In reality there is only one Ace (the chosen one) in the row – at the extreme left. *False shuffle the pack keeping the three Aces on top.*

"I will now deal three odd cards onto each Ace."

Suit your actions to your words by dealing three cards face down onto each card. The first three go on the left hand pile (**17, 18**), the second three on the next pile, and so on. The table now looks like this (**19**). Pick up pile number 1. Square the cards up and turn the pile face up – showing the chosen Ace – the Ace of Hearts (**20**).

"Let me put your Ace and the three odd cards into your pocket."

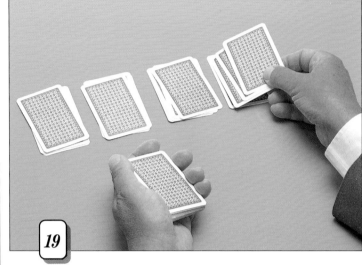

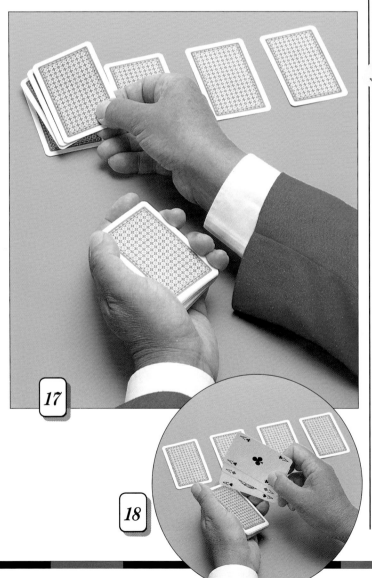

Be careful not to expose the other three Aces at this point. If he has not got a pocket, get him to stand up. Put the cards face down on a chair, then ask him to *sit* on the cards!

"Now watch very closely!"

Pick up one of the remaining piles and start to turn the cards face up, counting as you do so (**21**).

"One. Two. Three – odd cards. And an Ace."

21

22

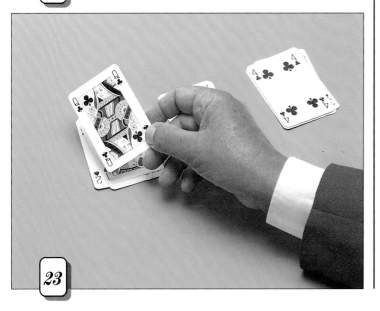

23

Turn the last card face up with a flourish (**22**).

"The Ace has gone!"

Repeat with the other two piles (**23**). Now all three Aces have mysteriously disappeared! Bring the trick to a stunning climax by having the spectator remove the four cards from his own pocket (**24**)! What has he got?

"The acrobatic four Aces!"

24

➤ AFTERTHOUGHTS ◄

Notice how the *false shuffle* enhances this trick. It subtly emphasises the apparent randomness of the odd cards that are used to cover the four Aces. Part Three of this book contains a collection of self-working tricks – in other words, tricks that require no sleight-of-hand for their performance. Once again our fabulous false shuffle can be used to enhance many of these; in the process, turning them from perplexing puzzles into outstanding magical effects.

AMBITIOUS CARD TRICK

This is a "classic" card trick. Audiences love to see it because so many "magical" effects are created within it. It is fast and furious card magic at its best! From our point of view, it gives you a marvellous opportunity to practise your skills of false shuffling, double lifting, gliding and general card control. I guarantee that somebody will say,

"Wow! I wouldn't like to play cards with you!"

◆ EFFECT ◆

A freely chosen card keeps repeatedly returning to the top of the pack – no matter how often the pack is shuffled.

REQUIREMENTS
A pack of cards
A spectator

◄ WHAT YOU DO ►

Spread the pack out and have the spectator choose a card (**1**). Make sure he remembers what it is otherwise you will feel very foolish. Have the card returned to the pack (**2**) and, in the process of an overhand shuffle, control it to the top. False shuffle keeping his chosen card on top (**3**). Flip the top card face upwards with a flourish to show his card (**4**)! (*First effect*).

Turn it face down, false shuffle again (**5**), flip the top card over to show that it has again returned to the top (**6**)! (*Second effect*).

Turn it face down. Undercut the pack. Run one single card on top of the chosen card, then injog the next card (**7**), shuffle off the rest, undercut at the injog and throw the block on top.

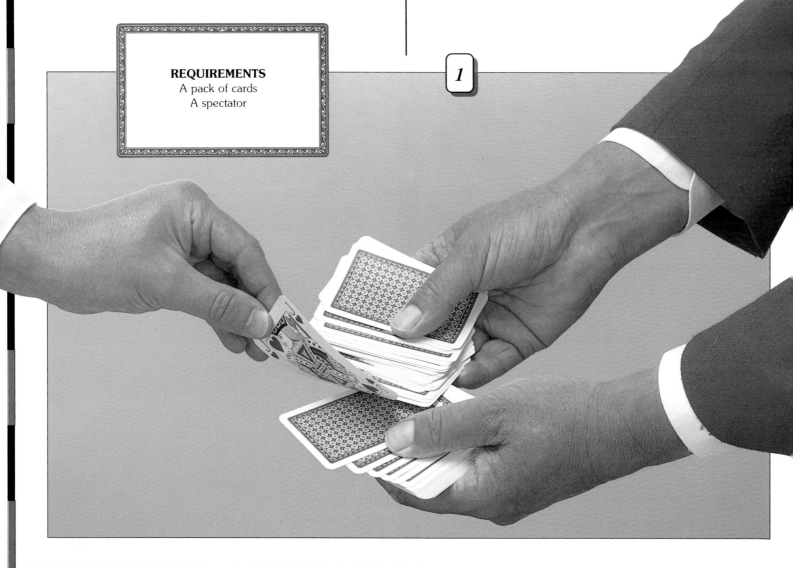

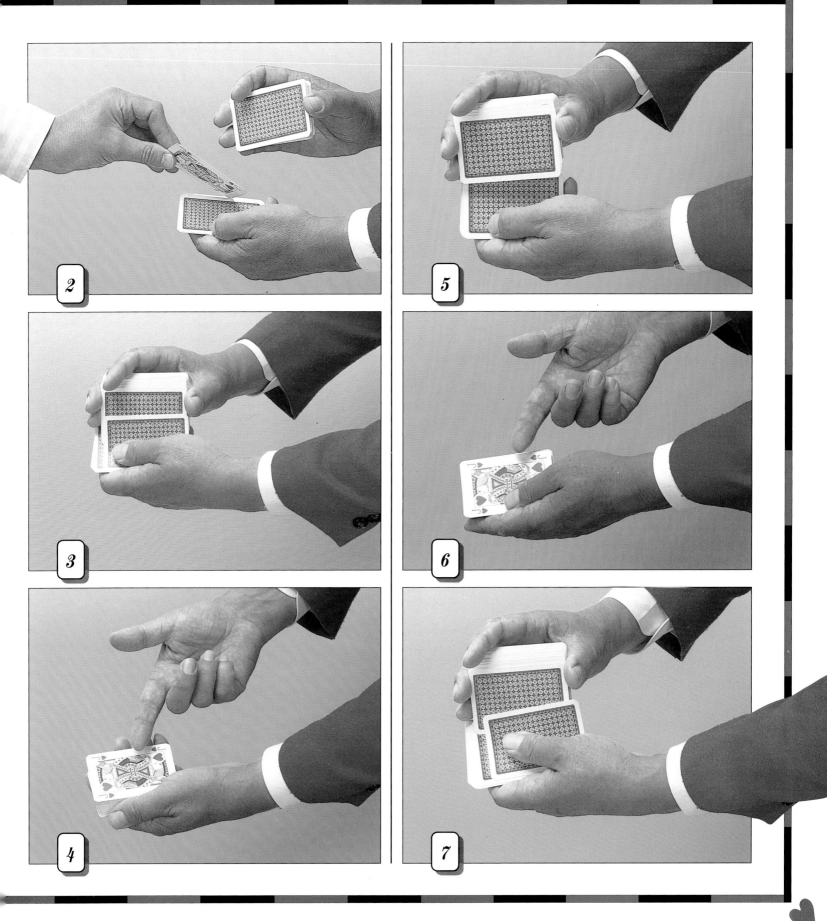

The spectator's card should now be second from the top! *Double lift* (**8, 9**) to show his card is back on top again (**10, 11**)! (*Third effect*).

Replace the two cards (**12, 13**). Take off the top card only (**14**) and, without showing its face, bury it somewhere in the centre of the pack (**15**). Make a flourish with your right hand, then turn the top card over (**16**). His card is back! (*Fourth effect*).

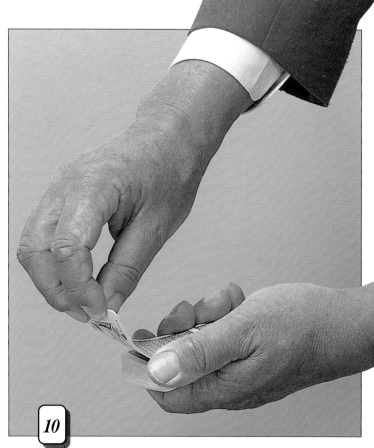

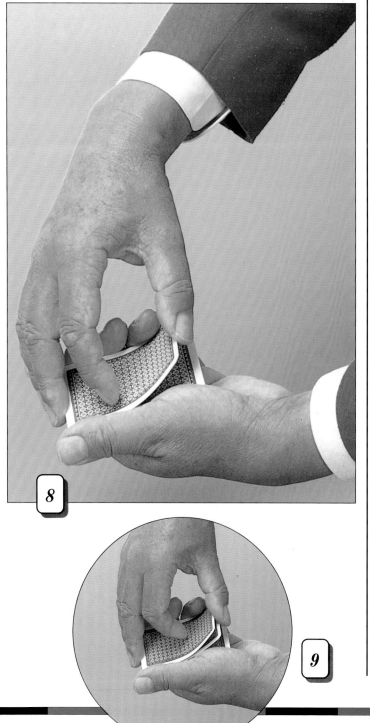

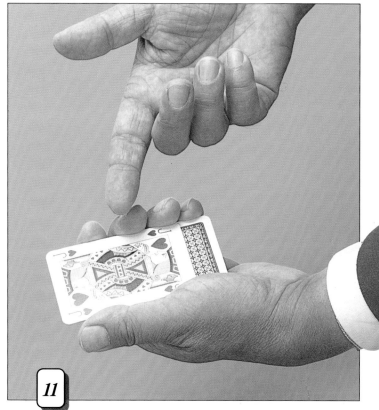

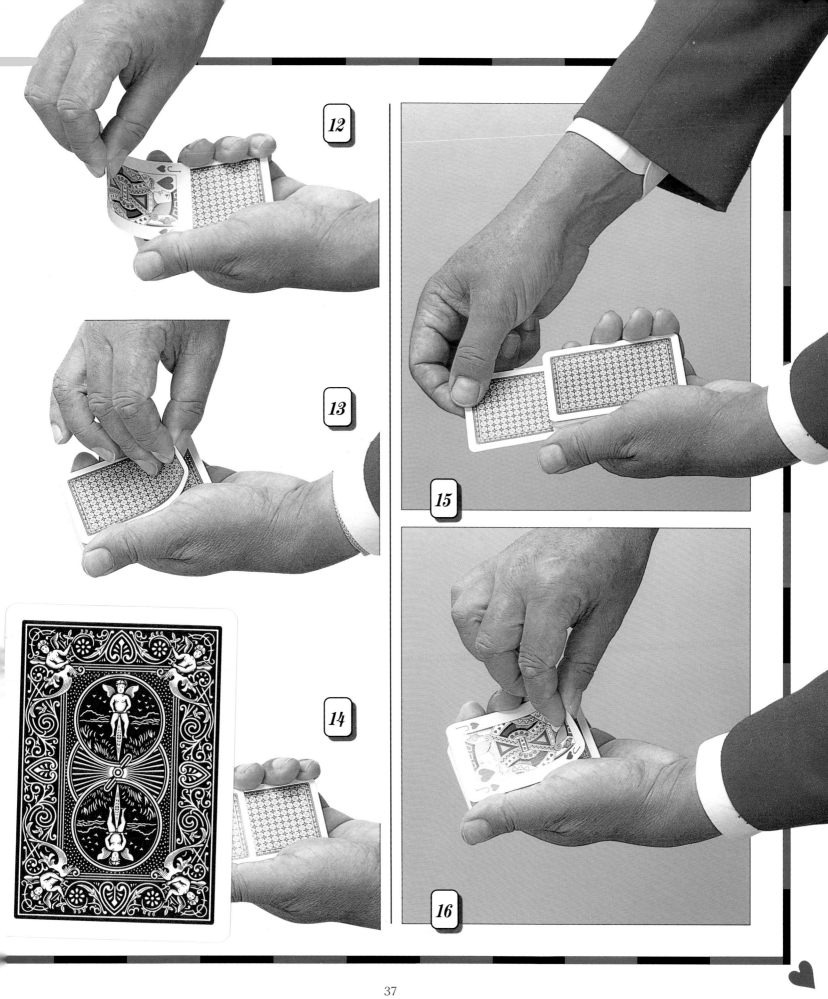

Put it face down on top again. This time false shuffle his card to the *bottom* (**17, 18**). Turn over the top card. Act surprised that it is not his card (**19**). Then slowly turn the whole pack over to show his card resting on the bottom (**20, 21**)! (*Fifth effect*).

Twist your wrist so that the pack is turned face downwards. In the process, execute *the glide* and apparently deal his chosen card face downwards off the bottom of the pack onto the table (**22**). Now false shuffle the deck to bring his chosen card to the top (**23**). Place the pack face down on the table (**24**). Bring the routine to a startling climax by showing that his chosen card is *not* the single card that you dealt down (**25**). Once again his "Ambitious Card" has risen to the top of the pack (**26, 27**)! (*Sixth effect*).

So there you have it. A dynamic card trick with no less than *six* strong surprises built into it. No wonder it has been a favourite of magicians for over a hundred years!

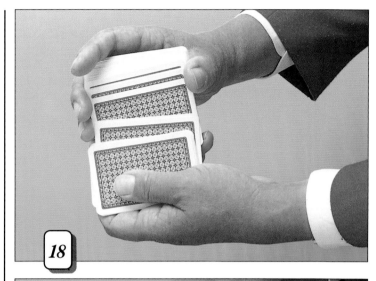

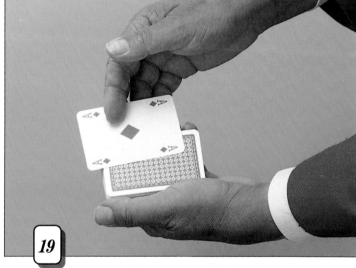

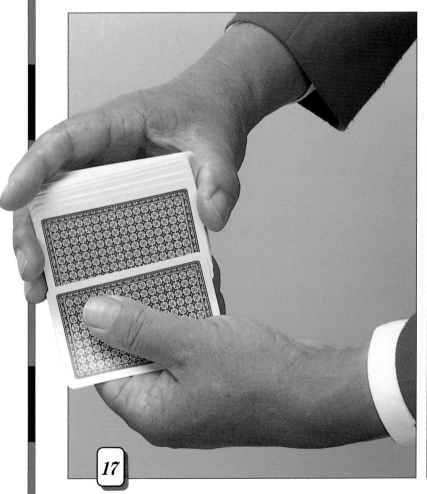

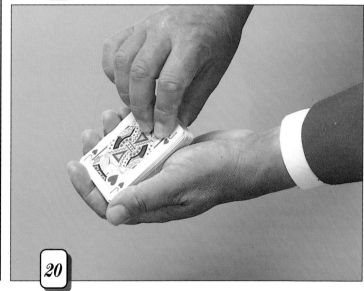

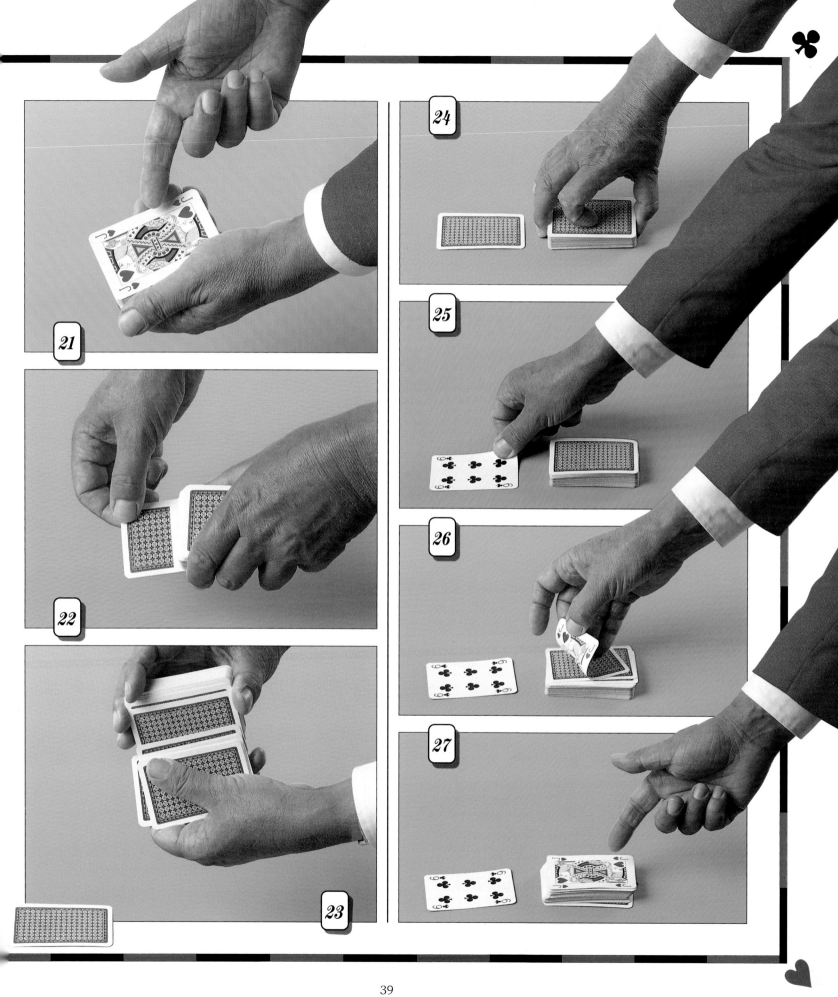

HERE TODAY – GONE TOMORROW!

Any trick where the "magic" happens in the hands of the spectator has got to be good. The effect this trick has upon the spectator is *dynamic*! The plot is good, the method very simple and the handling extremely deceptive.

◆ EFFECT ◆

A card is selected and returned to the pack, which is then shuffled. An indifferent card is then placed on a spectator's palm. The magician then says that by tapping the pack three times on the back and then three times on the front, the spectator's chosen card will magically reverse itself in the pack. After tapping, he fans out the pack face upwards and one card is seen to be reversed. The spectator is asked to reveal the identity of his chosen card for the first time, and then the magician turns over the reversed card. It turns out to be *not the selected card, but the indifferent card that the spectator is supposed to be holding*! The spectator turns over the card in his hand and is dumbfounded to find that he is holding *his own selected card*!

REQUIREMENTS
A pack of cards and the assistance of a spectator

❮ WHAT YOU DO ❯

Have a card chosen and returned to the pack (**1, 2, 3**). In this case it is the three of Clubs. Control it to the top during the course of an *overhand shuffle* (**4**).

Explain that during the shuffle his chosen card may have arrived at the top of the pack. Execute a *double lift* (**5, 6**) and lay the card(s) face up on top of the pack with its right long edge overlapping the pack by about 2cm (**7**). In our demonstration the visible card is the Queen of Diamonds (**8**).

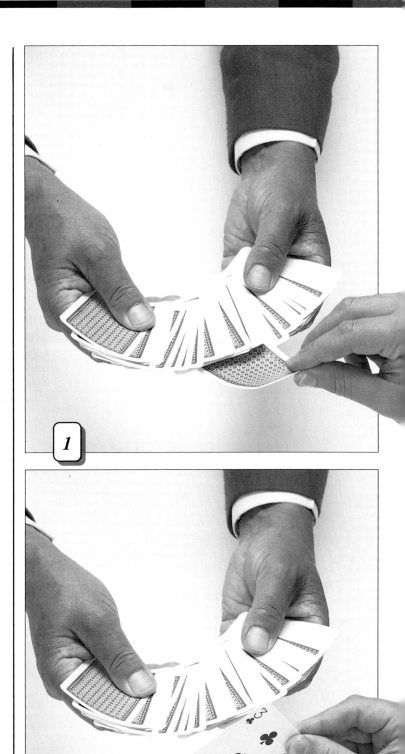

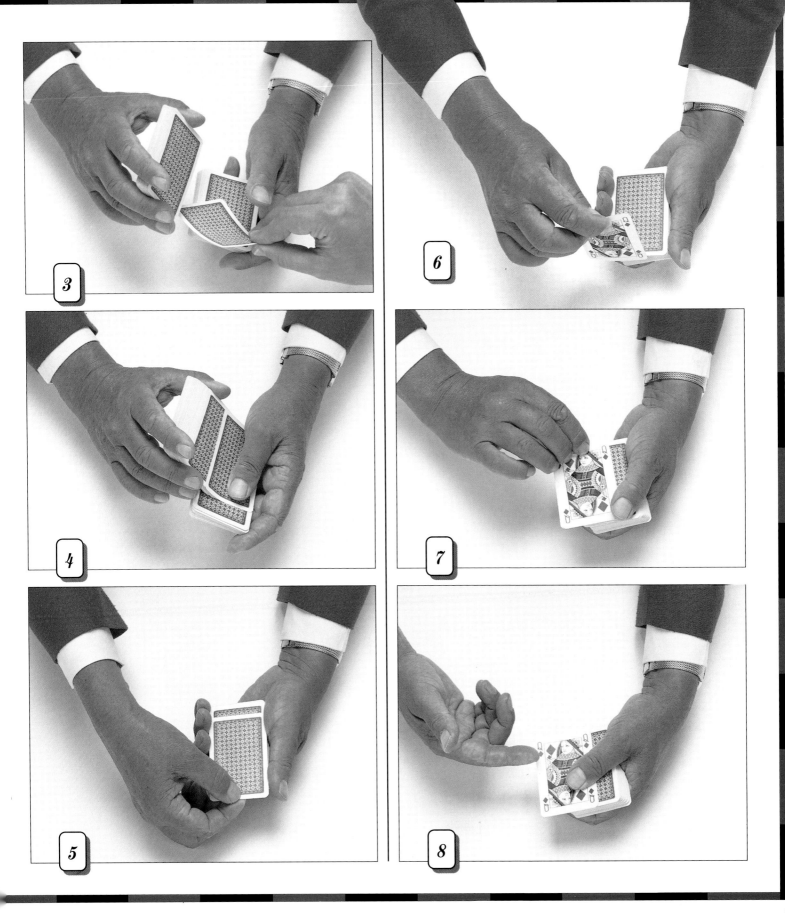

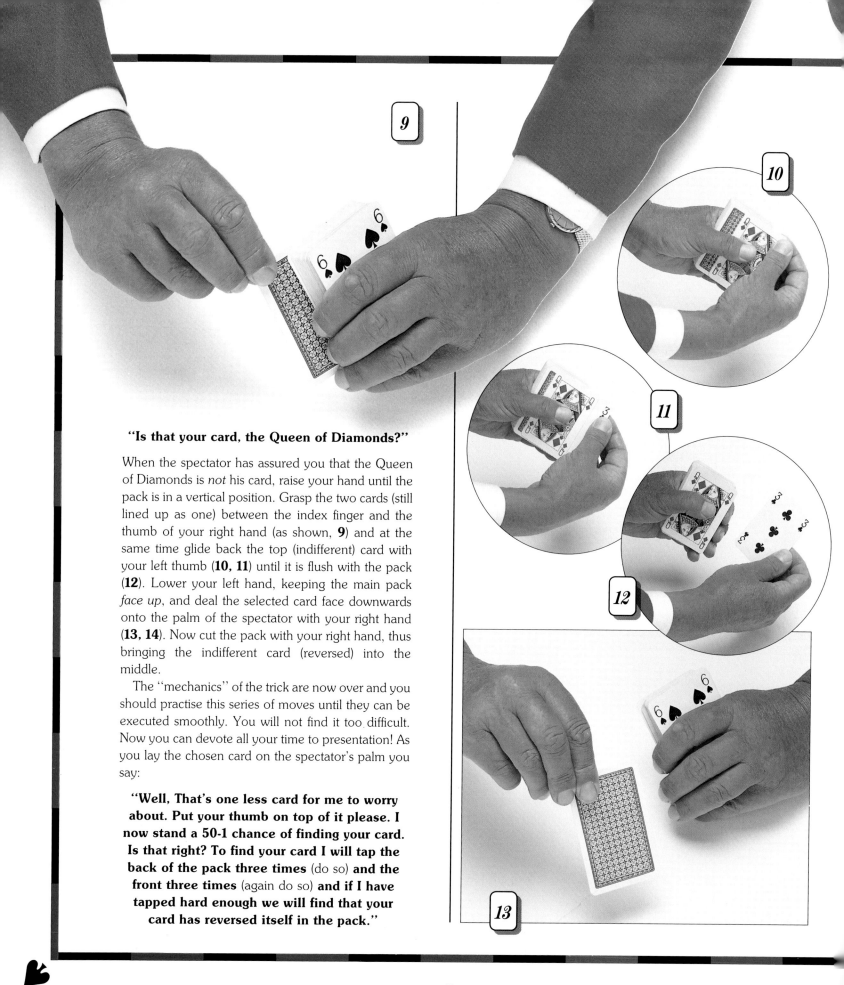

"Is that your card, the Queen of Diamonds?"

When the spectator has assured you that the Queen of Diamonds is *not* his card, raise your hand until the pack is in a vertical position. Grasp the two cards (still lined up as one) between the index finger and the thumb of your right hand (as shown, **9**) and at the same time glide back the top (indifferent) card with your left thumb (**10, 11**) until it is flush with the pack (**12**). Lower your left hand, keeping the main pack *face up*, and deal the selected card face downwards onto the palm of the spectator with your right hand (**13, 14**). Now cut the pack with your right hand, thus bringing the indifferent card (reversed) into the middle.

The "mechanics" of the trick are now over and you should practise this series of moves until they can be executed smoothly. You will not find it too difficult. Now you can devote all your time to presentation! As you lay the chosen card on the spectator's palm you say:

"Well, That's one less card for me to worry about. Put your thumb on top of it please. I now stand a 50-1 chance of finding your card. Is that right? To find your card I will tap the back of the pack three times (do so) **and the front three times** (again do so) **and if I have tapped hard enough we will find that your card has reversed itself in the pack."**

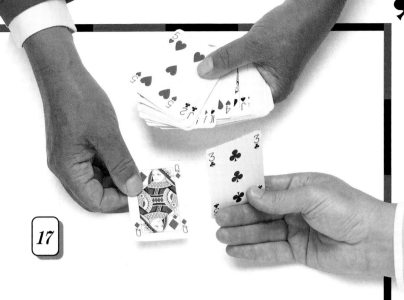

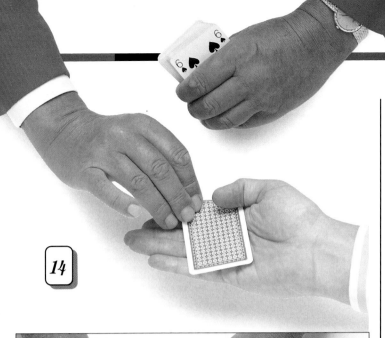

14

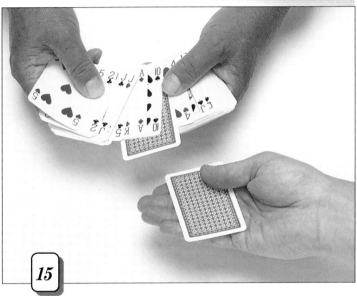

15

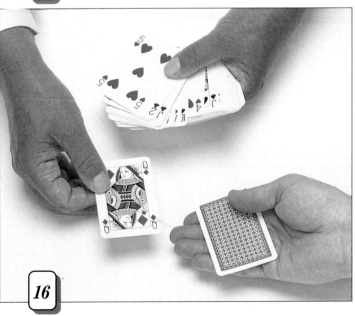

16

17

18

Fan the cards *face upwards* (**15**). Draw attention to the one reversed card. Take it out and hold it up without showing its face for the moment.

"It seems that I have been successful. You are holding the Queen of Diamonds; what was the card that you chose?"

He says it was the three of Clubs. Turn the card that you are holding over to show that *you* are now holding the Queen of Diamonds (**16**)!

"Well, I've now got the Queen of Diamonds which you are supposed to be holding! What have you got?"

He turns over the card that has been on his palm all this time (**17**) and finds to his amazement that he is now holding his chosen card, *the three of Clubs* (**18**)!

CARDS ACROSS

Because playing cards are fairly small they are not normally used by stage and cabaret magicians. This trick is a notable exception. It is an impromptu trick that you can present absolutely anywhere. It will have the same remarkable effect whether your audience consists of one or a hundred and one people.

◀ EFFECT ▶

You use two assistants. Each deals out ten cards and then stands on them. You make three cards magically jump from beneath one spectator's foot to reappear under the other spectator's foot! One now has seven cards – the other has thirteen!

> **REQUIREMENTS**
> A pack of cards
> A small table or stool
> Two spectators (we will call them
> Suzy and Kate).

♣ WHAT YOU DO ♣

Stand Suzy to your right and Kate to your left. The small table is in front of you. Turn to Suzy.

"Can you count to ten?"

"Of course I can."

"Education is a wonderful thing, isn't it?! You must have gone to a private school. I want you to count ten cards out loud onto the table like this . . ."

Demonstrate by dealing and counting about three cards onto the table by way of illustration (**1**). Then gather up all the cards again and give them to Suzy (**2**).

"Off you go – ten cards please – out loud – onto the table."

Suzy deals out ten cards (**3**) and is left holding the rest. Pick up the ten cards as you say

"I'll just check that you have counted correctly."

Count them yourself from hand to hand (**4**) and, as you square them up, get a little finger break under the top three cards. Push them slightly forward in preparation to palm them but *don't do anything else at the moment.* The timing of the palm is critical and, providing that you synchronize the following actions, it will be beautifully deceptive.

"Suzy, you were only *just* absolutely correct! You were nearly wrong! Give the rest of the cards to Kate . . ."

Just as she reaches across to do this, *palm the three cards in your right hand* (**5, 6, 7**).

8

9

Your left hand goes forward and across your body with the remaining seven cards (in a block) as you say (**8**)

". . . and put your ten cards on the floor over there and stand on them – preferably using your foot!"

She takes the cards from you and follows your instructions (**9, 10**). Your right hand, with the three cards secretly palmed, comes to rest casually by your hip. This natural action gives perfect cover for the palmed cards! Turn to Kate.

"Kate, I want you to do the same. Count ten cards onto the table (11) – out loud so that we can all hear you."

Our next "task" is secretly to add the three palmed cards to her pile of ten cards without anybody realizing. Once again the timing is all important! I will divide this sequence into three phases, A, B and C. (**A**) With your left hand, gesture to any free surface on your left, (such as another table, a chair or a sideboard) and say (**12**)

10

"Would you please put the rest of the pack over there, out of the way . . ."

(**B**) At the same time as she turns to do this (**13**), you push the ten cards (the ones she has just dealt) forward a little with your right hand, secretly adding the three palmed cards to the top of this uneven pile in the process (**14, 15**).

The extra cards will never be noticed. As you do this, you say (**16**).

". . . and then take your ten cards, put them on the floor over there . . ."

Gesture to a spot to your left (**17**) with your now empty *right* hand (**C**)

". . . and stand on them (**18**)."

I have separated these three stages intentionally. Practise the moves and try to get a *rhythm* going. A *slow* "A – B – C". The naturalness of these actions creates the deception. It is bare-faced cheek, really! Now, with the "dodgy bits" achieved, we must build the effect with *presentation*. Talk to Suzy again.

"I need a very long hair from your head!"

Reach up and *mime* plucking a hair from her head (**19**). Whatever you do, *do not* actually pluck a hair – just pretend! Pretend also that the hair just continues to come (**20**). The more you pull, the longer it gets! In fact it is so long that it reaches right across from Suzy's to *Kate's* head! Mime the act of fixing the end of the

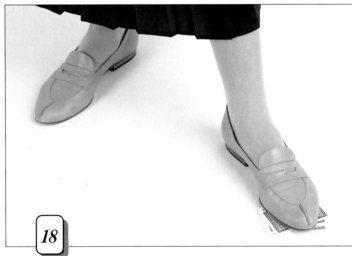

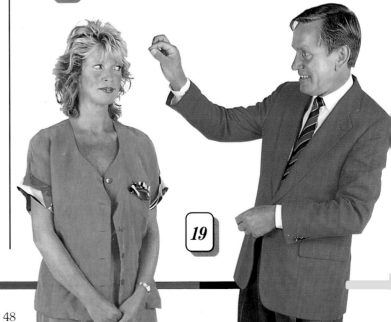

hair to Kate's head (**21**)! When I present the trick, I use an imitation mallet made from sponge rubber to hammer the end of the hair home! I give the lady a couple of gentle taps on the head with it! All good fun!

You have created a bizarre, farcical situation. Two grown-up people each standing on ten cards and joined together by an invisible hair (**22**)! Only a magician could get away with it! Hold your hands in a praying position:

> **"You are now joined together by holy hairlock! Now, this is the trick. Under your foot, Suzy, are ten cards. Under your foot, Kate, also ten cards and in between you is this incredible invisible hair!**
>
> **I will now make three cards fly from your pile, Suzy. They will travel up your leg, up your back and onto your head. Then, without the aid of a safety net, they will crawl slowly across the invisible hair until they reach your head, Kate! They will travel down your back and down your leg until they arrive on the pile of cards under your foot! They will travel over one at a time, and the first one will go now!"**

Pretend that you can actually *see* the first card leaving Suzy's pile (**23**), and travelling upwards onto her head. "Trace" its course across the invisible hair onto Kate's head (**24**), then down her body to her foot (**25**).

"Did you feel it arrive, Kate?"

She will think you have gone out of your mind!

"That was the first one! Let's try the second!"

Trace its invisible path as before.

"That's two. Now the third card is *really* difficult!"

Act as if you really have a struggle to make the last card manoeuvre its invisible course. Once it has apparently arrived under Kate's foot, breathe a sigh of relief

"Wow! That was very tricky! Now Suzy, if this trick has really worked, you would not have ten cards under your foot would you? You would only have seven. Pick them up from under your foot, bring them over to the table and count them out loud onto the table."

Suzy counts out her cards and is amazed to find that she now has only *seven* (**26**). Have her check beneath her foot once again to make sure that there are not any cards stuck to her foot! Turn to Kate.

"If this crazy trick has worked, Kate, you would not have ten — you would have the extra three to make thirteen! Bring them over here and slowly count them out loud so that we can all hear."

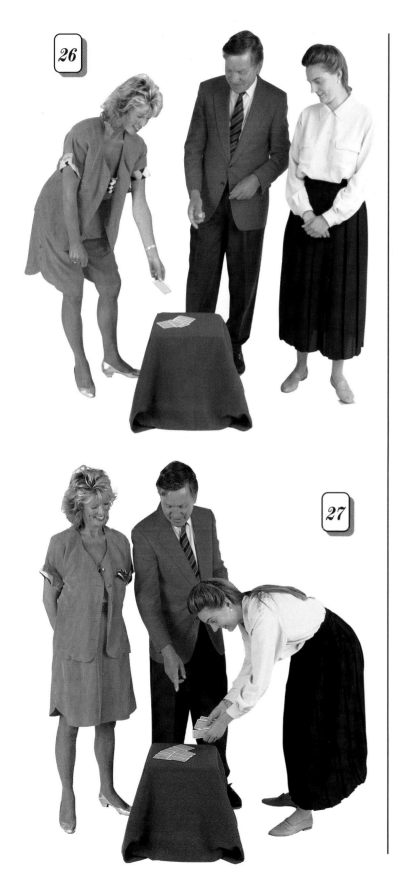

You join in as she counts. Count even louder when she reaches **"Eleven. Twelve. Thirteen."** This strongly emphasizes the appearance of Suzy's three cards (**27**)!

➤ AFTERTHOUGHTS ◀

Well, there you have it. A zany, very entertaining card routine that really packs a punch at the end (**28**). Nor is it difficult to do, once you have got the hang of the timing. Notice how the simple act of palming three cards results in a chance for you to indulge in some delightful humour. It is a great exercise in *presentation*. The patter that I have given you *is* funny. However, I would suggest that you adapt it to suit your own personality. If you use words and phrases that you would not normally use in everyday speech, your performance will become stilted and less convincing. Never be afraid to introduce ideas of your own. That is how new tricks are born.

THE PIMPERNEL QUEEN

This famous trick, usually called "Find the Lady", has a chequered history. It is a racetrack swindle. Basically the idea is that you have to find the Queen which is one of only three cards used. The three cards are shown face up, you are asked to note the position of the Queen. The cards are then turned face downwards and very slowly mixed around. You (the "mark") are invited to say which one of the three face-down cards is the Queen. The only problem is that you are asked to put your money where your mouth is and back up your choice with hard cash!

Needless to say, you always lose. You may see someone else win and thus be encouraged to try your luck too! Beware! The winner that you saw was "in" on the scam – a member of the gang – he is known as a "shill". Two or three more members of the team will be positioned around to keep an eye out for the police so that a quick getaway can be made if it becomes necessary! So the racket is "feeding" at least four people and is, of course, strictly illegal.

Even to this day you will come across gangs fleecing unwary people at racetracks and even on the city streets with "Find the Lady". It is also sometimes known as "The Three Card Trick" or "Chase the Ace". If you ever come across such a team please keep your money in your pocket – cross the road – walk away – do not get involved. This simple gambling game is not a "game" at all, but an outright con. There is no way for you to win. The operator ("thrower") of the cards will be an extremely expert sleight-of-hand merchant! You have been warned!

Magicians always cheat fairly! I will now teach you an entertaining routine that has been inspired by the traditional racetrack swindle although the methods that we will use will be very different! Your audience will credit you with having incredible skill! I call it The Pimpernel Queen.

REQUIREMENTS
Two identical Queens
Three identical Jokers
One trombone-type wire paper clip
Double-sided adhesive tape

♣ EFFECT ♣

While performing a "Find the Lady" routine, the Queen repeatedly disappears only to be found in the performer's pocket! Even with the restraints of a paper clip placed upon her, the Lady vanishes yet again!

◆ WHAT YOU DO ◆

Stick a Joker and a Queen together, *back to back*, using the double-sided tape. Glue would do, but the sticky tape gives a better finish (**1**). Put the ungimmicked Queen in your right hand pocket. Place the double-faced Joker/Queen between the two ordinary Jokers with the Queen side showing.

Lay the three cards on the table (**2**).

"This is a trick called 'The Pimpernel Queen'. I use two Jokers . . ."

Pick up the two Jokers and hold them face up in your left hand.

" . . . and a Queen."

Pick up the Queen (being careful not to "flash" its Joker side) and place it next to the two Jokers (**3**).

"You must keep your eye on the Queen at all times. Are you watching?"

Close up the small fan and in so doing get a little finger break under the top two cards (the double-sided Queen and the first unprepared Joker) (**4**). Push them forward (**5**) and then turn both cards face downwards as one (**6, 7**).

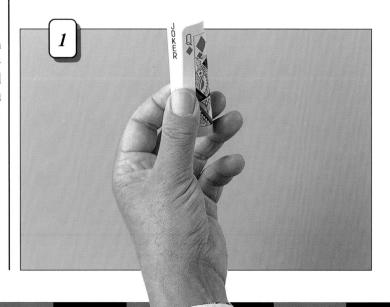

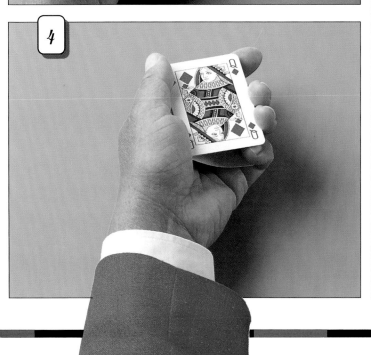

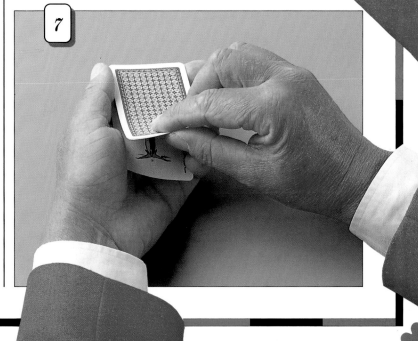

♥

Now spread the cards out again (**8**). Apparently the Queen is now face downwards on top. Actually, the back that can be seen is the back of the Joker. Our double-faced card is now in the middle with its Joker face showing and its Queen face hidden! Transfer the face-down card to the centre of the spread (**9**). Now address one of the spectators and say,

"No matter how I mix the cards up now, you will have no problem keeping track of the Queen because it is the only face-down card! Take out the Queen for me please. Turn it over."

He does so (**10**) and is flabbergasted to find that it is not the Queen but another Joker (**11**)!

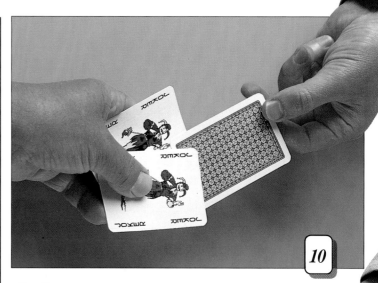

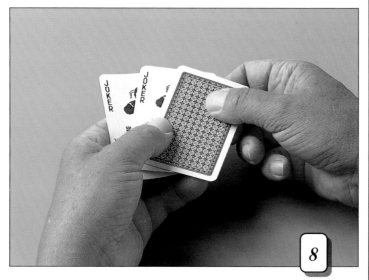

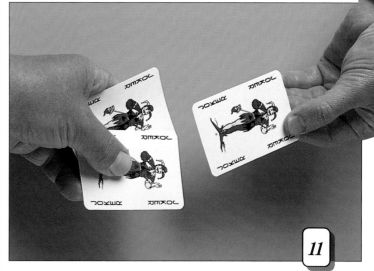

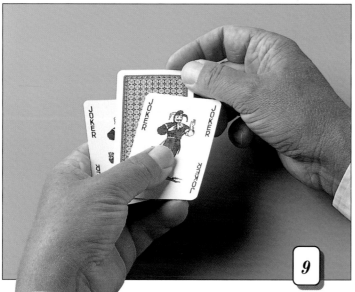

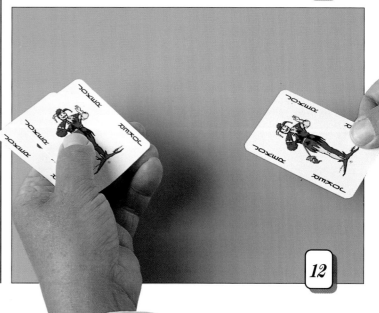

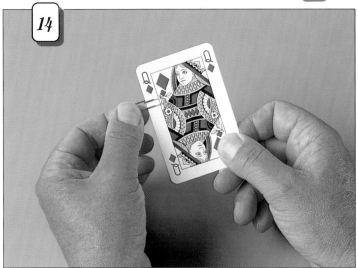

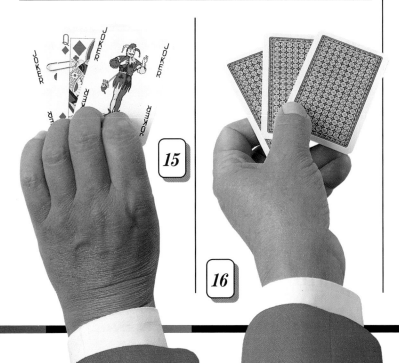

"I had another Joker in my pocket and, when you were not looking, my hand shot into my pocket like a flash with the Queen and changed it for the Joker!"

As you say this, pick off the top Joker (**12**) (really the double card), put it, and your hand, into your pocket and turn the double card over bringing the same card out again only with its *Queen* face showing again (**13**)!

"I'll do it again!"

Repeat all the previous moves, but this time when your hand goes to your pocket with the double card, *leave it there and bring out the ungimmicked Queen which you previously placed there*! You are now, as we say, "clean"! You now add an *extra* refinement by introducing the paper clip.

"Just to help you keep track of the 'Pimpernel Queen' I will put a paper clip on her."

Slip the paper clip on the long side of the Queen (**14**) and then hold the three cards in your left hand as shown, with the paper-clipped Queen in the middle (**15**). It is important that the cards are held *exactly* as shown. The first two fingers are placed near the lower left corner of the top card and the thumb immediately behind. The three cards are first shown face up, and then face down by turning the hand over (**16**).

Show them face up and then face down again. Now remove the card immediately under your thumb (Joker) and place it face downwards on the table to your right (**17**). This leaves two cards in your hand.

"If I place a card over there . . ." (gesture towards the tabled card) **". . . what cards have I got left? Yes, that's right, the Queen with the clip and the Joker."** (Show their faces, **18**) **". . . and the card over there is a . . . ?"**

You distract the spectator's attention by asking this question and pointing to the card on the table again. As soon as he looks towards the card, turn your left hand over (**19**), bringing the two cards into a face-down position, *and at the same time* twist your two fingers and thumb that are holding the cards so that the two cards slide past one another (**20**) and change positions (**21**). As this happens, the Joker will automatically engage the clip and "steal" it from the Queen (**22**)!

This is a very sweet move and with a little practice you will soon get the hang of it. The transfer of the clip from one card to the other is disguised by the greater movement of the hand as it turns the two cards face downwards. The eye is incapable of taking it all in at once. Place the newly clipped card onto the table (**23**) and tell your chosen spectator to keep his eyes firmly on it.

Now lay the card without the clip (Queen) on top of the free card on the table and in the same action pick them both up and put them away in your pocket (**24**).

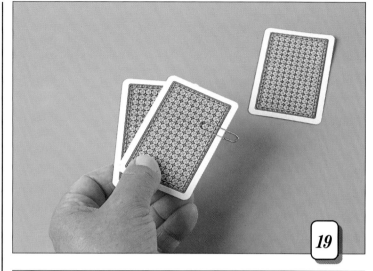

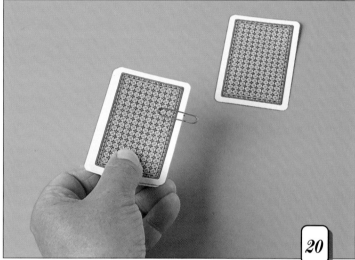

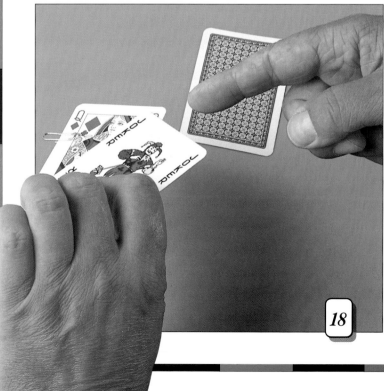

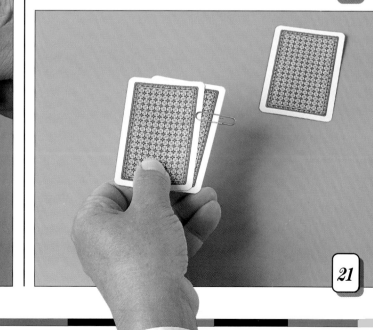

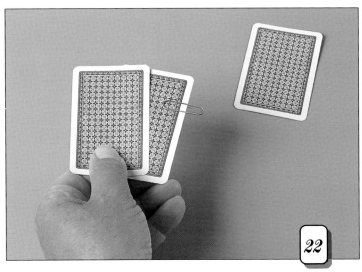

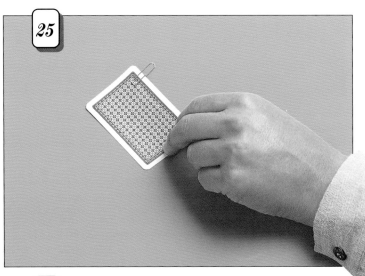

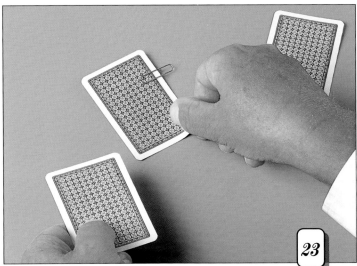

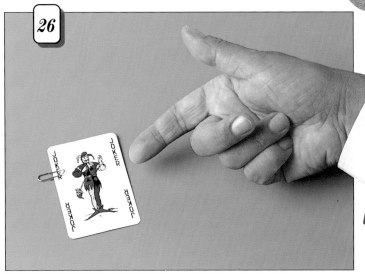

"I'll just put the Jokers in my pocket out of the way. Do you know why I call her 'The Pimpernel Queen'?

**They seek her here,
They seek her there,
They seek her almost everywhere!
Is she in heaven?
Is she in hell?
That darned elusive Pimpernel!**

Turn her over please!"

He turns over the card with the paper clip (**25**) and finds, to his utter astonishment, that the Pimpernel Queen has flown! The Joker (that's you) has the last laugh (**26**)!

CHANGE OF IDENTITY

This is a cute, snappy trick with some remarkable magical changes actually happening in the hands of two spectators!

◀ EFFECT ▶

Two spectators each hold a card. On your command the cards change places!

REQUIREMENTS
A pack of cards
One extra card (say an Ace of Spades)
Two spectators (we will call them Kate and Suzy)

▶ WHAT YOU DO ◀

Arrange the pack so that the top three cards are: Ace of Spades, Queen of Hearts, Ace of Spades (**1**). Put the cards in the case and the case back in your pocket.

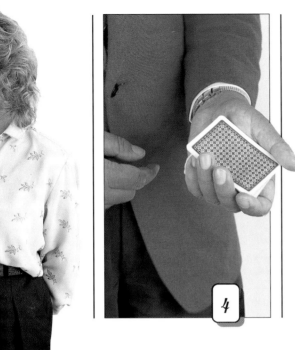

Stand Kate to your right, Suzy to your left. Take out the case, remove the cards (**2**) and *return the empty case to your pocket* (**3**). This is important – you will see why later. Give the pack a couple of *false shuffles* keeping the top three cards in place. Secure a little finger break under the top *two* cards (**4**) in preparation for a *double lift*. Turn to Kate (**5**).

"What is your name?" "Kate." **"Well, Kate, I am going to change your identity!"**

Double lift, showing the Queen of Hearts (**6**) and lay the two cards, (still aligned) on top of the pack (**7**).

"From now on you are going to be Miss Queen of Hearts (8)!"

Turn the two cards face downwards again (**9, 10**) and deal the top card only (Ace of Spades) (**11**) onto Kate's outstretched palm. Have her cover the card with her other palm (**12**). She thinks it is the Queen of Hearts!

"What is your name now?" "Miss Queen of Hearts" says Kate. **"That's right!"**

Give the cards another couple of false shuffles and then prepare for another doubt lift as you turn to Suzy.

"What is your name?" "Suzy." Double lift showing the Ace of Spades (**13**). **"From now on you will be known as Miss Ace of Spades! O.K.?"**

Turn the card(s) face downwards as before and deal off the single top card onto Suzy's palm (**14**). Have her cover it with her other hand too (**15**). It is really the Queen of Hearts but she *thinks* it is the Ace of Spades. The reason for asking them both to hold their respective cards sandwiched between their palms in this way is to stop them fiddling with them and exposing their faces prematurely. This would rob you of the climax that you are working up to.

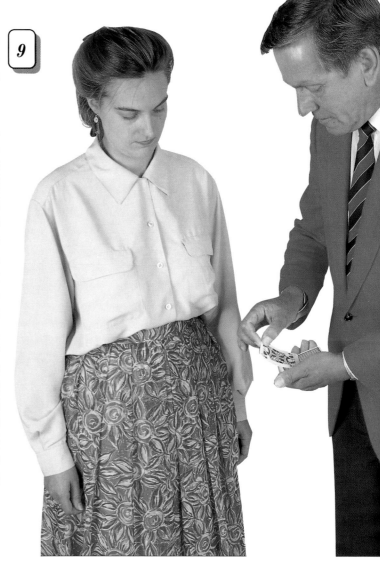

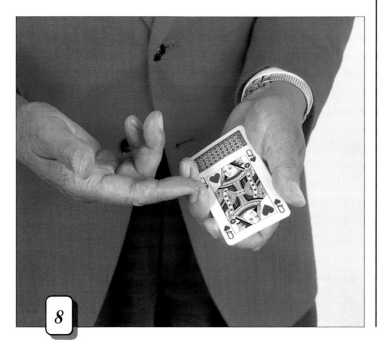

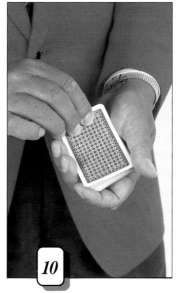

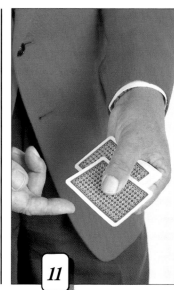

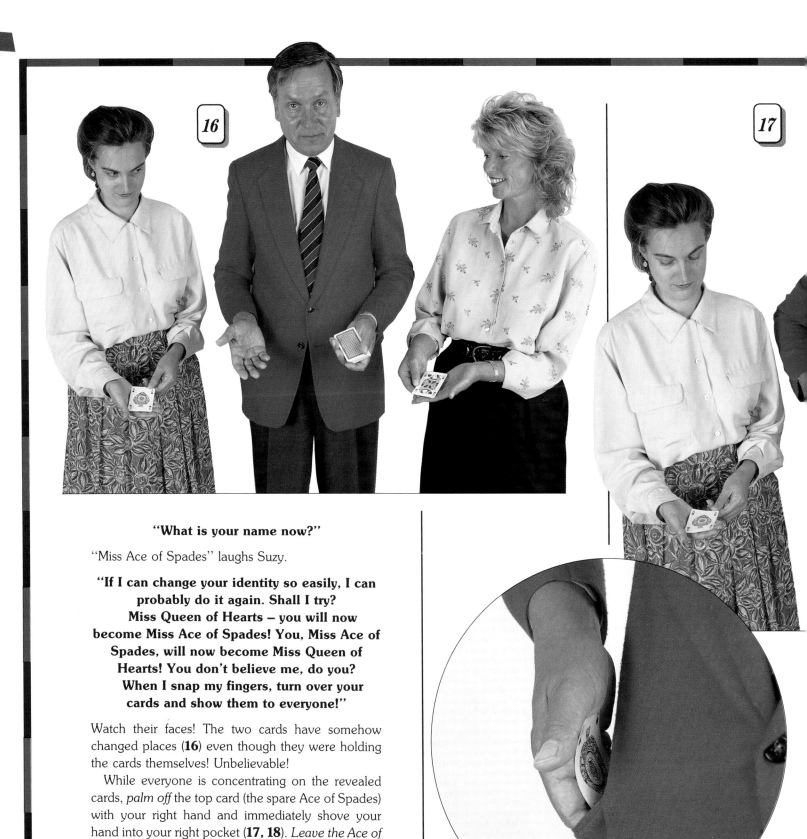

"What is your name now?"

"Miss Ace of Spades" laughs Suzy.

**"If I can change your identity so easily, I can probably do it again. Shall I try?
Miss Queen of Hearts – you will now become Miss Ace of Spades! You, Miss Ace of Spades, will now become Miss Queen of Hearts! You don't believe me, do you? When I snap my fingers, turn over your cards and show them to everyone!"**

Watch their faces! The two cards have somehow changed places (**16**) even though they were holding the cards themselves! Unbelievable!

While everyone is concentrating on the revealed cards, *palm off* the top card (the spare Ace of Spades) with your right hand and immediately shove your hand into your right pocket (**17, 18**). *Leave the Ace of Spades there* and bring your hand out again holding the empty card case. Put the cards into the case (**19, 20, 21**) and then casually toss it onto the table. If anyone should want to examine the cards later, all is now "clean"!

◆ AFTERTHOUGHTS ◆

Like all the best tricks, this one has a very simple plot and is quite easy to do. We magicians often put thoughts into the minds of our audiences. Notice how the two false shuffles very subtly emphasize the apparent fairness of it all, so that at the end there is no logical explanation. It must be magic!

Although, at the end , the pack may be examined by any curious spectator, *you should not openly invite such scrutiny*. It is bad psychology and puts the wrong type of thoughts in people's minds. The pack should be above suspicion. We remove the extra card so that, should you wish to perform another trick, you will not be embarrassed by the sudden appearance of five Aces! People have been shot for less!

THE PHOENIX CARD TRICK

This trick will ruin two cards. Having said that, I think you will find that it has such a fantastic effect upon the spectators that you will consider it worth the expense. I keep two packs of cards aside just to enable me to perform this trick. That's how good *I* think it is.

♣ EFFECT ♣

A card is selected and torn up. One corner piece is given back to the spectator, who then sets light to the rest of the pieces! In a flash, the destroyed pieces reappear inside your wallet which has been on the table throughout. To cap it all, the corner that she has been looking after fits perfectly!

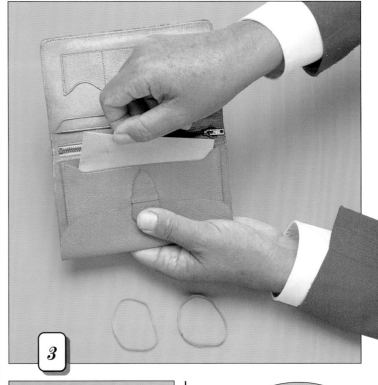

REQUIREMENTS

Two cards the same (say both eight of Hearts)
Your "working" pack of cards
A wallet
Two rubber bands
Two good quality thick envelopes

Matches and a large ashtray
A spectator (we will call her Jill)

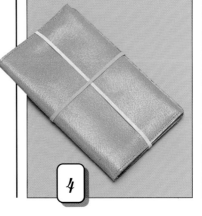

♣ PREPARATION ♣

Tear a corner off one of the cards so that it looks like this (**1**). Seal the rest of the card inside one of the envelopes (**2**) and place it inside your wallet (**3**). Place a rubber band around the wallet (one each way) effectively "locking" it (**4**).

Hide the piece that you tore off the eight of Hearts in the corner of the other envelope (**5**). *Do not seal it down.* Place the other eight of Hearts on top of your pack. Put the pack back in its case. Before you start, the loaded wallet, the envelope containing the hidden corner, the pack of cards in its case, the matches and the ashtray should all be ready on the table.

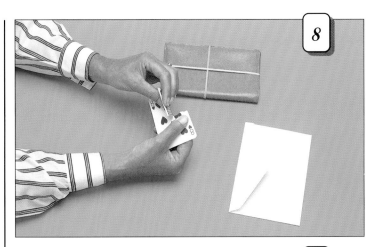

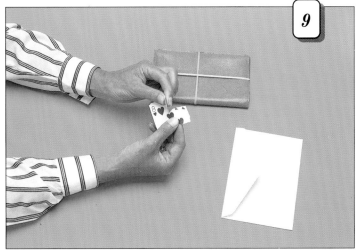

➤ WHAT YOU DO ◀

Take the cards out of the case and give them a quick *false shuffle*. Now force the eight of Hearts (**6, 7**). I would suggest that the *slip cut force* is probably the best one to use for this trick. Try to give the impression that the choice of the card is of no real significance to you.

"I want you to tear your card into eight pieces. I know it will ruin the card but don't worry, there's no expense spared when I'm around!"

While she does this (**8, 9**) , pick up the envelope and hold it in readiness as shown with your fingers inside concealing the spare corner that you previously placed there (**10**).

"Drop the pieces into this envelope please, Jill."

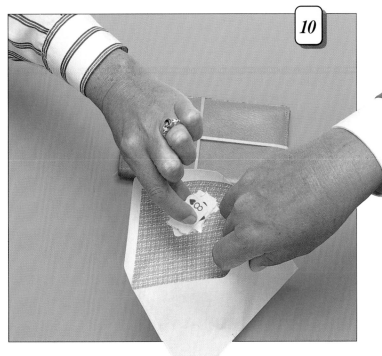

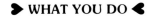

As soon as she has dropped the pieces into the envelope begin to lick the flap to seal the envelope down. Then before you press the flap down, and *almost as an afterthought*, take out the extra piece and give it to Jill to look after (**11**).

"Please look after this bit until the end, Jill"

Now seal the envelope, pick up the matches and set fire to it. It is best to start at one corner and let the flames lick up the sides of the envelope (**12**). It goes without saying that you do this over the large ashtray that you have readily at hand. Try to reduce the whole thing to ashes (**13**). You must ensure, at the very least, that all the pieces of torn card are completely destroyed. Once the flames are out and things have cooled down, pick up a handful of ash and crumble it between your fingers (**14**).

"You know, Jill, nothing in this world is ever completely destroyed. Even this card. It is now floating through the air invisible to the human eye. In this state, however, it is possible to resurrect the card. Watch!"

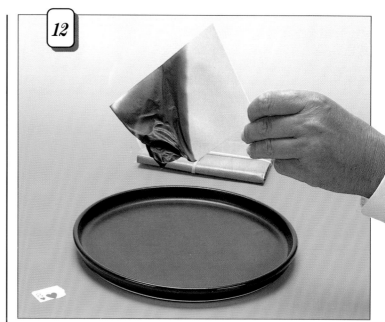

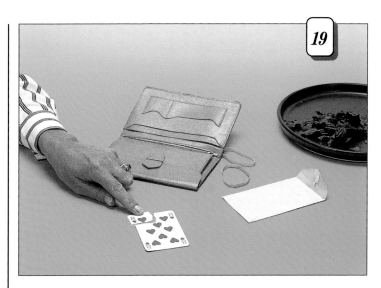

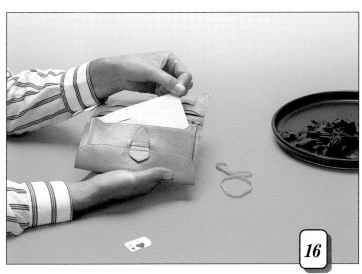

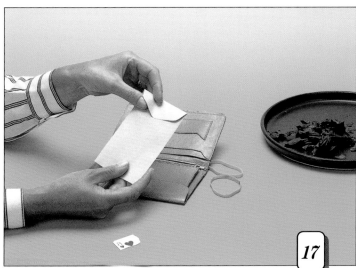

Grab handfuls of fresh air and make magic passes with them towards the wallet, which you will remember has been in full view throughout.

"This is called the Phoenix Card Trick. Your card, like the mythical bird, has now risen from the flames and is completely restored! Open up my wallet. Remove the sealed envelope from inside and see what it contains!"

Jill does all this (**15, 16, 17**) and finds the "restored" eight of Hearts (**18**). Minus one corner!

"See if the corner that you kept fits the gap, Jill."

She does (**19**). It does(**20**)!

THE GHOSTLY CARD!

The time that you have spent learning to false shuffle and palm cards will be rewarded once you have mastered this beautiful trick. It is very popular among card magicians.

◆ EFFECT ◆

A spectator freely chooses a card, returns it to the pack and then shuffles the cards himself. You wrap the cards in a handkerchief and hold the parcel high in the air. The spectator names his card and you gently shake the parcel. His selected card is seen slowly to penetrate through the handkerchief, finally being shaken clear and falling to the floor. The rest of the pack is still securely wrapped up in the handkerchief!

This short description cannot hope to do justice to this fine trick.

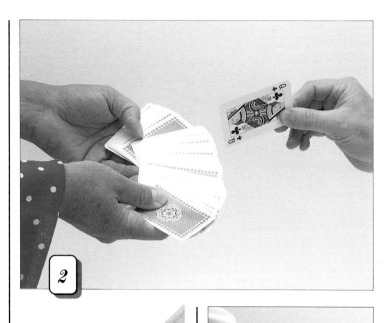

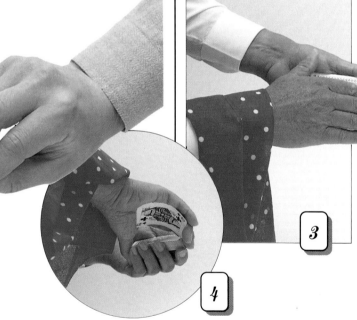

REQUIREMENTS
A pack of cards
A clean, good quality handkerchief
A spectator (we will call him Paul)

♣ WHAT YOU DO ♣

Drape the handkerchief over your right arm, waiter fashion! Have Paul choose a card (**1**) and remember it. Have it returned to the pack (**2**) and then control his card to the top of the pack during the course of an overhand *false shuffle*. Prepare to palm his card off the top. *Do not do it yet!*

Please don't forget the name of your card, Paul. To be absolutely fair, I'd like you to give them all a good shuffle too!''

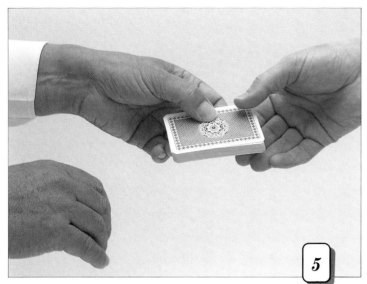

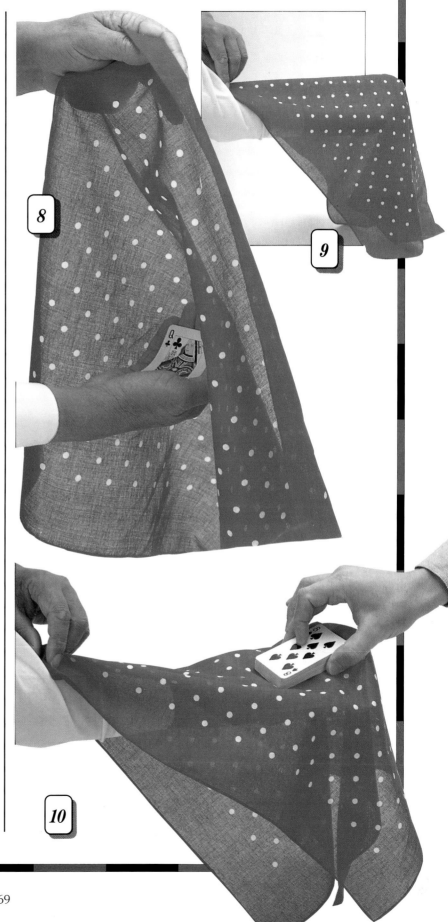

Paul will look at your face as soon as you start to talk. *Palm the card now* (**3, 4**), taking the rest of the cards away with your left hand and giving them to him to shuffle (**5**). As soon as he has taken the cards, remove the handkerchief that is hanging over your arm (**6**) and drape it over your right hand (**7**). In the same action, turn the hand palm upwards (**8**) and cover your hand with the handkerchief (**9**). *These four actions that must be practised until they flow and blend into one.*

"Paul, now that you have shuffled the cards, I want you to place them face up on top of the handkerchief (10)."

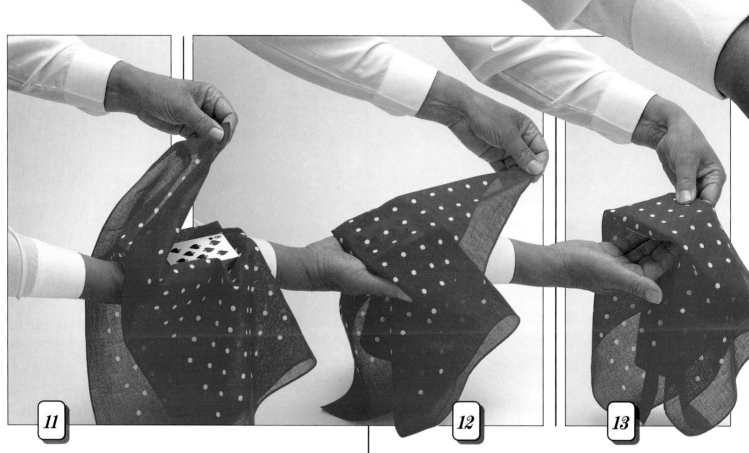

He does this. You now have to wrap the cards up in the handkerchief. It is very important how you do it. The end result will be that the pack will be on the *inside* and the palmed card will be on the *outside*!

With your left fingers pull the fold of the handkerchief that is draped over your right wrist *forward* (**11**) to cover the cards (**12**). Take a grip on the pack, the handkerchief *and* the hidden card beneath it, with your left fingers as illustrated (**13**). You can now take your right hand away.

The left and right sides of the handkerchief are hanging down on their respective sides. Fold these sides down and underneath the pack and take any surplus material forward, twisting it rope fashion (**14**). The pack should now look like this (**15**). This is an exposed view and not one that is seen by the spectators. The parcel is now casually shown on both sides. Your right fingers cover the otherwise visible end of the selected card! Hold the twisted part of the package in your left hand at about head height (**16**).

"What was the name of the card you chose, Paul?"

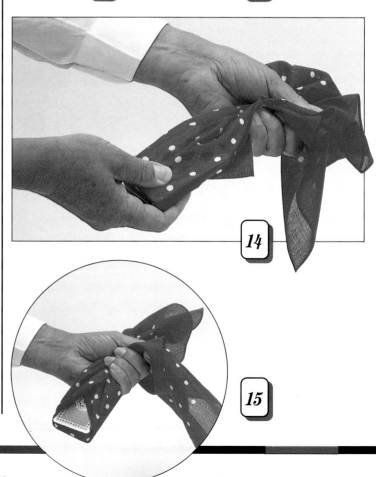

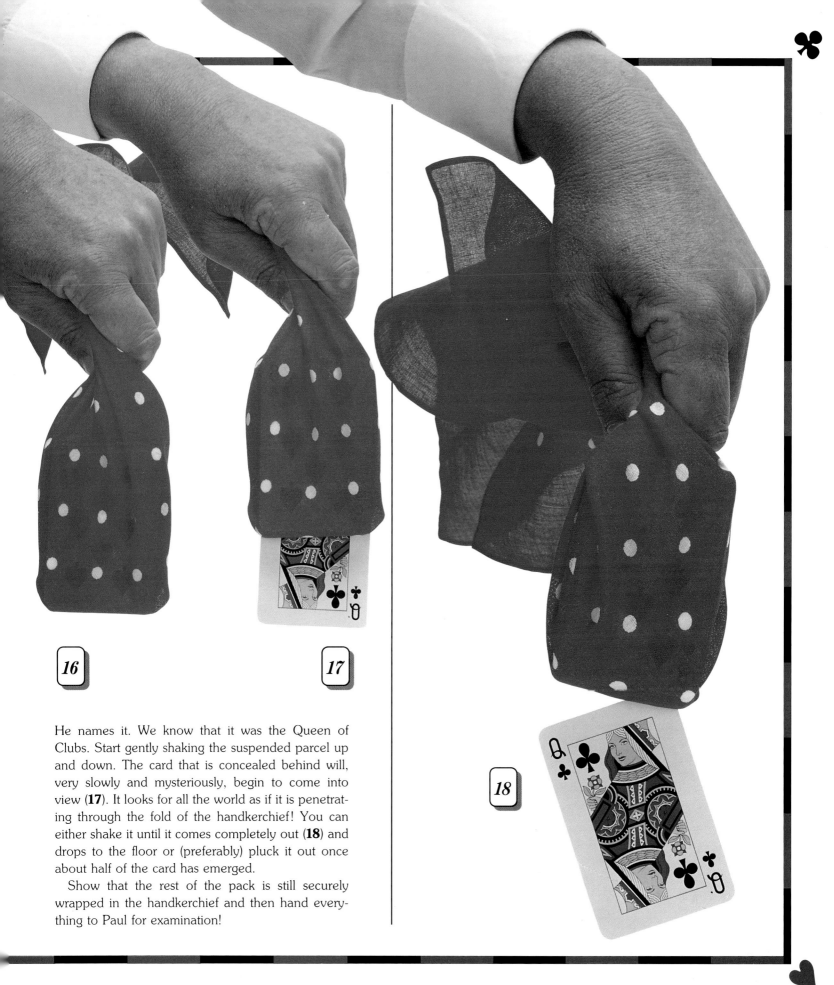

16

17

18

He names it. We know that it was the Queen of Clubs. Start gently shaking the suspended parcel up and down. The card that is concealed behind will, very slowly and mysteriously, begin to come into view (**17**). It looks for all the world as if it is penetrating through the fold of the handkerchief! You can either shake it until it comes completely out (**18**) and drops to the floor or (preferably) pluck it out once about half of the card has emerged.

Show that the rest of the pack is still securely wrapped in the handkerchief and then hand everything to Paul for examination!

CLEOPATRA'S NEEDLE

This spectacular trick ruins a card each time you perform it – so use your own pack, not a borrowed one. You do not want to lose your friends, even in the cause of magic!

◆ EFFECT ◆

A freely chosen card is shuffled back into the pack which is then wrapped up in a paper parcel. The spectator is invited to stick a darning needle (that has been threaded with ribbon) into the edge of the pack at any point that he wishes. It is pushed right through and out the other side, thus threading the ribbon through at the same point.

The spectator holds each end of the ribbon with the paper parcel suspended from its centre. He is asked to name his card (say the two of Clubs). The paper is now ripped away. All the cards drop to the floor – all that is except his chosen card, the two of Clubs! It remains suspended with the ribbon penetrating right through its centre!

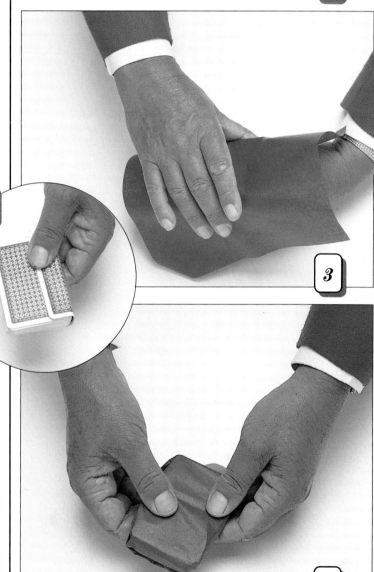

> **REQUIREMENTS**
> A pack of cards
> A sheet of coloured paper
> The longest darning needle that you can find
> Approximately 1 metre of ribbon
> (red looks best)

You hold the parcel while he does this (**7**). Offer him the clear long edge first and help him guide the needle into the parcel and then out the other side. Make sure that he realizes that you are in no way trying to influence where he puts it. He will not notice the slight extra pressure needed to push the needle through the other side. Pull the needle completely through (**8**) and keep pulling until the paper package reaches the centre of the ribbon. Then remove the *needle* completely.

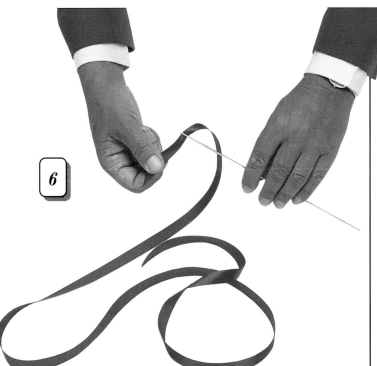

◆ WHAT YOU DO ◆

Pick your spectator. Let us call him Oliver. Have him choose a card (**1**), look at it and remember it (**2**).

Always emphasise that a card should be remembered. You would feel very foolish if you got to the end of the trick and the spectator could not remember the name of his card! I know! It has happened to me!

Get the card returned to the pack and control it to the top in the course of an overhand *false shuffle*. Now wrap the pack up in the paper (**3**). As you do so, slide the top card over and around the long side of the pack (**4**). You will find this quite easy to do – although a few practice rounds would be advisable to perfect your technique. The card should be slipped over *secretly* under cover of the wrapping process (**5**) and will not be suspected.

"Now Oliver, take this darning needle (6) and stick it into the parcel. I want it to go through the paper, pass between any two cards, and then come out the other side. In other words, I want you to thread the parcel onto the ribbon. Please mind my fingers!"

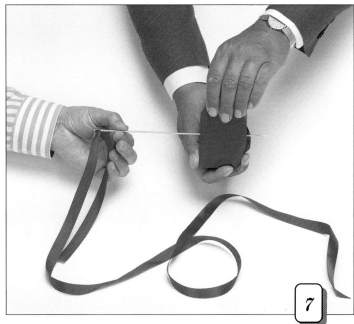

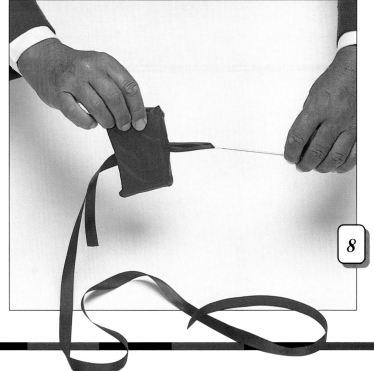

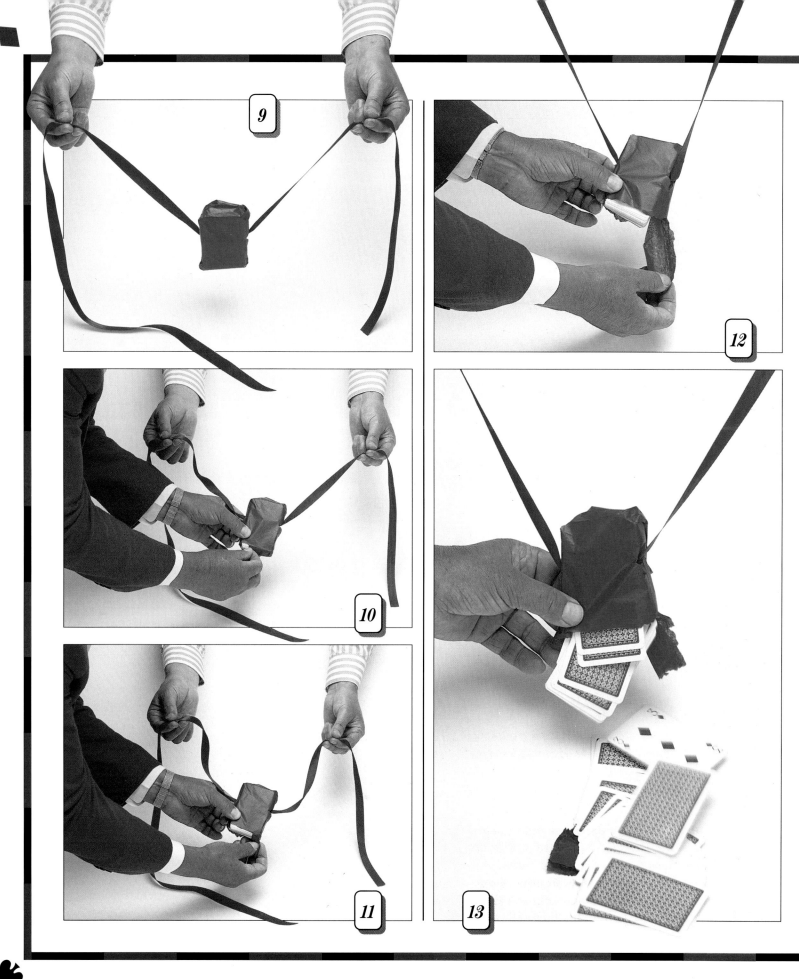

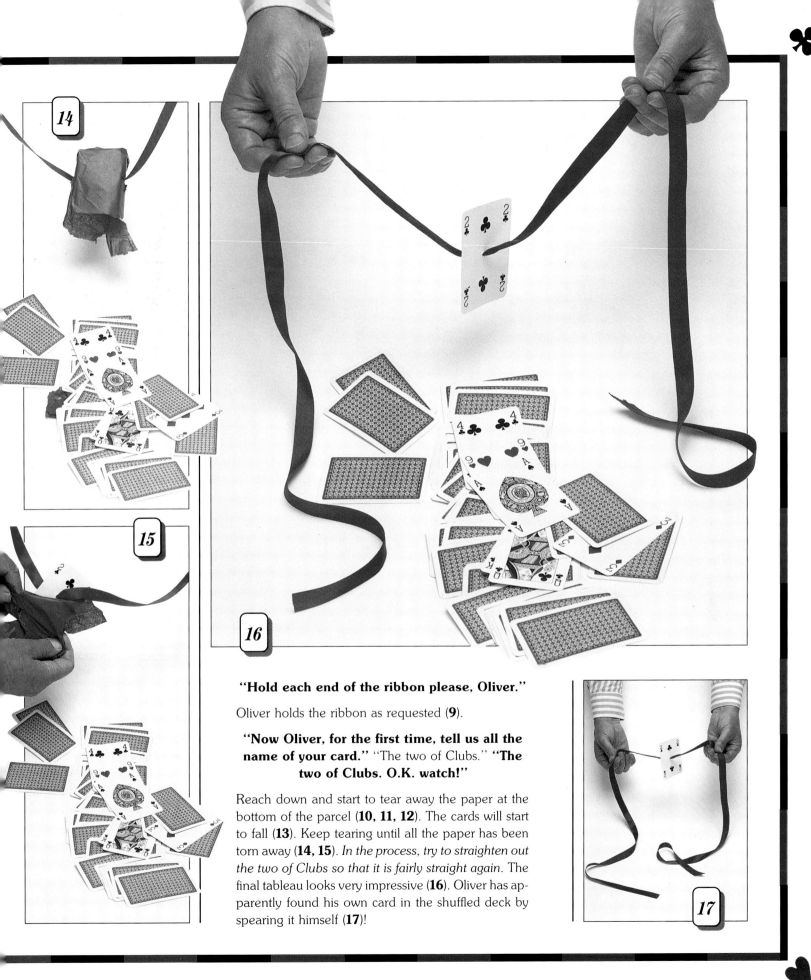

"Hold each end of the ribbon please, Oliver."

Oliver holds the ribbon as requested (**9**).

"Now Oliver, for the first time, tell us all the name of your card." "The two of Clubs." **"The two of Clubs. O.K. watch!"**

Reach down and start to tear away the paper at the bottom of the parcel (**10, 11, 12**). The cards will start to fall (**13**). Keep tearing until all the paper has been torn away (**14, 15**). *In the process, try to straighten out the two of Clubs so that it is fairly straight again.* The final tableau looks very impressive (**16**). Oliver has apparently found his own card in the shuffled deck by spearing it himself (**17**)!

THE GOBSMACKER CARD TRICK

Aﬀter performing this trick, your friends will think that you are totally brilliant, super skilful, and a Master Magician!

♣ EFFECT ♣

The name of a spectator's chosen card is found written on a piece of paper that is concealed in your shoe!

REQUIREMENTS
A pack of cards
A piece of paper bearing the
appropriate message

◀ PREPARATION ▶

Write these words on a piece of paper and sign it at the bottom:

**You are thinking of the Queen of Hearts!
signed Mystery Man**

Fold the paper up and slip it in your right shoe! Place the Queen of Hearts on top of your pack of cards and you are all set.

▶ WHAT YOU DO ◀

Get a volunteer. Let us call him Simon. Give the cards an overhand *false shuffle* retaining the Queen of Hearts on top. Now perform the *cross hand force* which, very effectively, forces the Queen of Hearts (**1**). Do not forget to emphasize the fairness of everything to Simon. (You cannot see the cards, he shuffles repeatedly, etc., etc.)

Ask him to remember the card (**2**) before he returns it and loses it in the pack when he shuffles them (**3**). Turn around to face him while he is still doing the final shuffle. Now we lead him up the garden path a little!

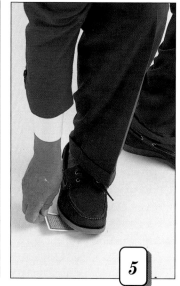

7

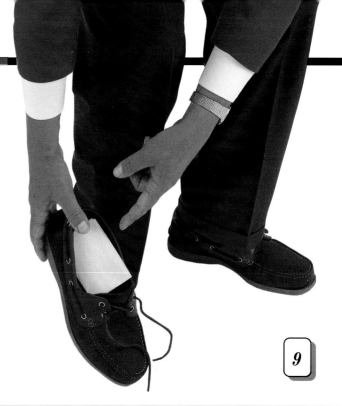

9

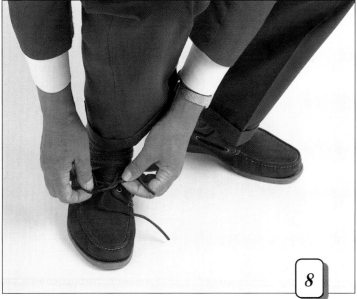

8

10

"You shuffled the cards, chose one, returned it to the pack and shuffled yet again. Obviously, Simon, nobody knows now where your card is, do they?"

He agrees that it would be impossible. Take the pack back and start to look through them as if you are trying to find his chosen one. Then, with a look of triumph on your face, take out any card (**4**) (*not* the Queen of Hearts) and, without showing it, place it face downwards *under* your right shoe (**5**).

"Your card is now under my right foot!"

(*Don't say "shoe"*). Pick it up (**6**). Turn it over (**7**) and say

"Tell me – yes or no – is that your card?"

"No."

"Oh dear! Can I try again?"

Take off your shoe (**8**), pick up the piece of paper (**9**), and give it to Simon to read out (**10**). *He will be absolutely gobsmacked!*

THE SEE-THROUGH CARD TRICK

If you are in the right place at the right time this classic of card magic is an absolute stunner! You will, however, have to choose your location and moment very carefully. Never attempt to do it unless the conditions are 100 per cent favourable. It is too good to be ruined by bad presentation.

◆ EFFECT ◆

A spectator chooses a card, returns it to the pack and shuffles the cards himself. You go to a window in the room and hold the pack against the window pane. The spectator is then invited to take your place, holding the pack in position. You walk a few paces away, turn and then ask the spectator to name his card. You ask the spectator to return the cards to you. He does, but he appears to leave one card stuck to the glass. It is his chosen card! You ask him to pull it off so that you may show it to the rest of the audience. To his utter amazement he finds that he cannot.

His chosen card is actually on the other side of the glass, outside the window!

REQUIREMENTS

The window must be suitable, with curtains that can easily be pushed aside. This is an "after dark trick". A duplicate of any card in your pack. We will assume that it is the five of Spades.

♣ PREPARATION ♣

Long before you do this trick you must stick the duplicate card to the outside of the window so that it faces inwards (**1**). A small piece of double sided sticky tape does the job nicely. If you are in an upstairs room and you have the opportunity secretly to open the window, you just reach around as far as you can, stick the card in position and then close the window and re-draw the curtain.

❯ WHAT YOU DO ❮

You start with the five of Spades on top of the deck. *False shuffle* a few times and then *force* the spectator to choose the five of Spades by your favourite method. The slip force or the cross hand force are both very suitable.

Once the spectator (let us call him Jim) has remembered his card, returned it to the pack and given it a shuffle, give the pack to him to shuffle too. This is

always a good policy when you do not have to keep track of a selected card. Just make sure he loses it in the deck. If you notice that he has shuffled the force card to the bottom ask him to give the cards another little shuffle!

"Let me have the pack now, Jim."

You take it from him and walk over to the window. Your left hand pulls the curtain to one side while your right hand (which contains the cards) quickly puts the pack directly over the card that is outside the window (**2**). Your back helps conceal what is actually happening and as Jim has no idea what you are trying to do, you will find it an easy matter to set yourself up in the correct position. The cards, of course, must have their faces towards the room.

"Now Jim, I want you to take over from me. Come and hold the cards against the window for me please"

You swap places (**3**) and walk a few paces away, then turn to face him.

"What was the name of the card that you chose?" "The five of Spades."
"Please bring the cards to me now, Jim."

He does so (**4**).

"Look Jim! You seem to have left one card behind stuck to the window. Good gracious! It is your card! The five of Spades . . . would you fetch it for me please!"

In a daze, Jim goes back to the window and tries to peel off his card (**5**). To his utter amazement he finds that, somehow, his chosen card has passed through the glass and is now on the *outside* of the window!

➤ AFTERTHOUGHTS ◄

Although I do not think it vital, if you have the opportunity during the mayhem to palm the other five of Spades and secretly pocket it, do so! An alternative "insurance" would be to keep the other pack of cards from which the duplicate card was originally moved in one of your pockets and just casually swap the packs as the spectator goes to retrieve his card from the window.

TIMES FOUR

This lovely routine is very close to my heart. It is well worth the practice and effort needed to perfect it. If you have digested the technical section at the beginning of this book you will be in possession of all the skills required to make this trick very special.

◆ EFFECT ◆

A pile of Aces instantly changes places with a pile of Queens, only a split second after all the cards have been shown!

❮ WHAT YOU DO ❯

Arrange the Aces and Queens as shown in the photograph (**1**), and spread them out across the table. Gesture towards the table.

"I have five Queens and five Aces – all left over from last night's poker game!"

Pick up a Queen from one end and an Ace from the other and lay them on the table just above the spread (**2**).

"These two cards will act as our 'markers'."

Scoop the rest of the cards up with your right hand *but* (apparently accidentally) miss the first two Queens – leaving them on the table (**3**).

"Oops! Sorry!"

Pick the last two Queens up and place them on top of the Aces (**4**) – *not in their original position!* This is a very casual, laid-back sequence of actions and should not attract suspicion. Turn the block of cards face down. Very slowly and deliberately deal the first four

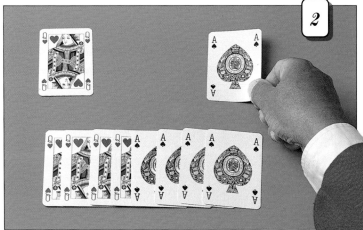

cards face downwards in a pile just beneath the Ace marker, counting them as you go (**5**). The first two will be Queens, so make sure that you do not inadvertently flash the faces of these to the audience. The third and fourth cards dealt are actually Aces, so you can flash the faces of these. Don't make a big thing of it – just be casual.

"We have one, two, three, four Aces."

Deal the remaining four cards face downwards beneath the Queen marker in the same way (**6**). As before, be careful not to flash the first two.

"And over here we have one, two, three, four Queens." Pause. **"Let's see what happens if we change the positions of our two markers!"**

Switch the two markers over so that the Ace is now above the left hand pile and the Queen above the right hand pile (**7**). Pick up the four cards from the left hand pile. Turn them face up and hold them in your left hand as shown (**8**). The spectator will probably be surprised to see the face of the Ace instead of the Queen that he was expecting!

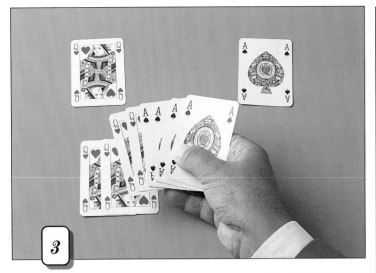

3

4

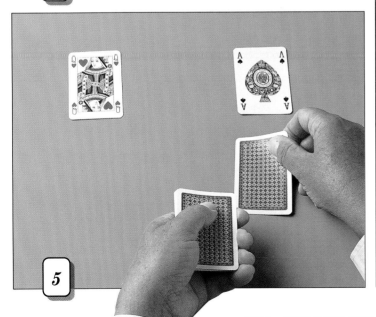

5

6

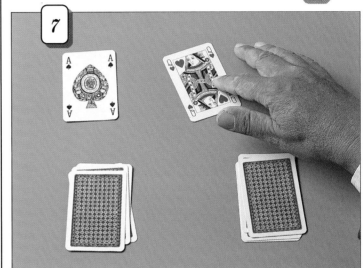

7

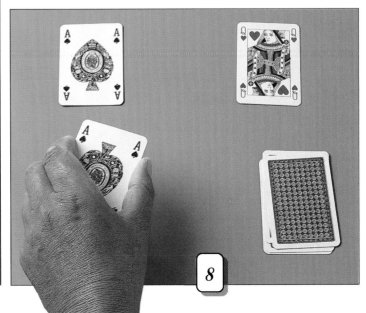

8

This next move has four separate parts which must blend into one. (**A**) With your right fingers and thumb pull the top Ace to the right until it is clear of the other three cards (**9**). (**B**) Turn your left wrist so that its cards are now face down (**10**). (**C**) Place the Ace in your right hand face downwards on top of these three face-down cards (**11**). (**D**) Twist your wrist back the other way so that the cards are face up again. You count . . .

"One."

All you have done is to transfer an Ace from the face of the packet to the back of the packet. You must do it exactly as I have described because next time we do it, although everything will *look* the same, we are actually going to cheat a little!

Secretly *glide* back the bottom card (**12**). Grip the remaining three cards as one and pull them to the right just as you did with the single card a moment ago (**13**). Turn your left wrist to bring its card face downwards (**14**). Deal the three cards (as one) face downwards upon it (**15**). Twist your wrist to bring the cards face up again (**16**). *This should look exactly the same as before.* You count . . .

"Two."

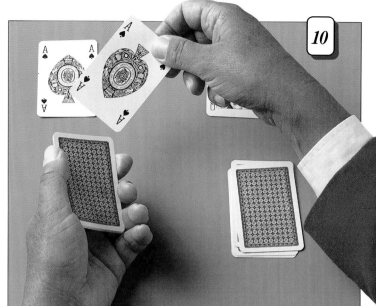

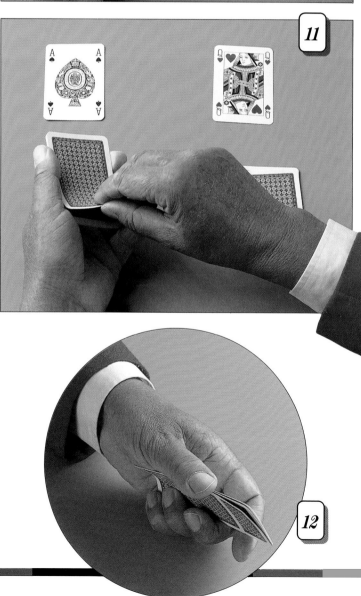

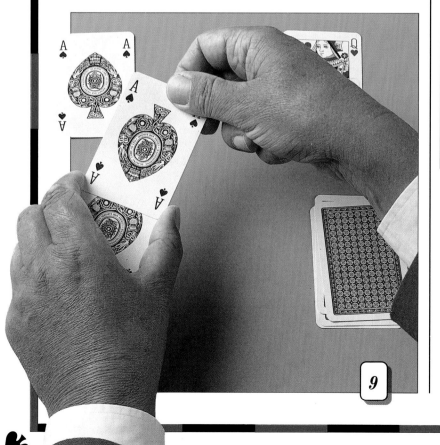

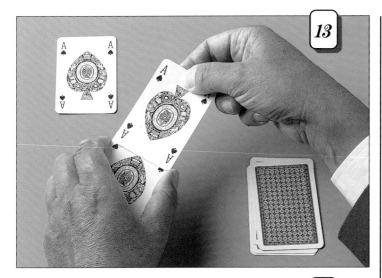

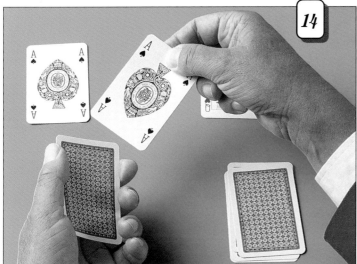

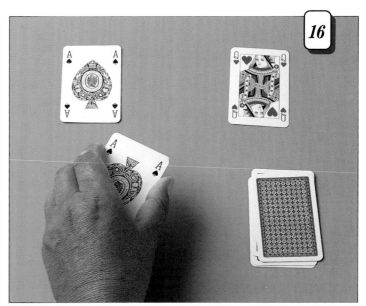

Now transfer a single card again as you count . . .

"Three"

. . . and finally do the *treble lift* version again as you count . . .

"Four Aces!"

Square the four cards up and place them *face up* beneath the Ace marker (**17**).

"Where we had the Queens, we now have the Aces . . ."

Pick up the left hand pile and repeat all the above sequences with these cards (**18-23**), showing that you have (apparently) *four Queens*!

". . . and where we had the Aces, we now have the four Queens."

Once you have shown them, place this pile face up *on top of the other pile* (**24, 25**). Pick up all eight cards, turn them face downwards and then start to deal them one at a time onto the table, counting them as you go . . .

". . . and all we use are the one, two . . ."

You break off after you have dealt the first two (**26**) and throw the remaining six cards on top of them (**27**).

". . . Oh! Here, examine and count the eight cards yourself!"

With this natural and casual action you destroy all the evidence because the eight cards are now back in their original order (**28**) and can be examined until kingdom come!

◆ AFTERTHOUGHTS ◆

For my money, this trick has everything. It has a simple plot, it is short, quite easy to do, and is extremely deceptive when correctly performed. It means having to buy a few packs of cards in order to get the cards necessary for the trick, but you cannot have everything, can you? You will find that, as a magician, you cannot have too many packs of cards either!

PART THREE

SELF-WORKING CARD TRICKS

THE DREAM CARD

I learned to do this trick forty years ago and still perform it today. Unlike me, it has aged very well!

❮ EFFECT ❯

The spectator finds *your* chosen card and yet has no idea how she does it! She handles the cards herself throughout.

REQUIREMENTS
A pack of cards

♣ WHAT YOU DO ♣

Give the pack of cards to the chosen spectator (we will call her Suzy) and ask her to give them a thorough shuffle.

> **"Last night I had a dream. In this dream I could see a playing card. Hold the pack up in front of me and pass them from one hand to the other, one at a time, so that I can see their faces. I want to find the card that I dreamed about. Just stop when I tell you."**

At this point you do not really have a card on your mind. Instead you pay particular attention to the *first two cards* that she shows you (**1**). They dictate which card you will pretend to be dreaming about. You use the *value* of the first card and the *suit* of the second card to determine your choice. For example: if the first card that she shows you in the *nine* of clubs, and the second the Queen of *Hearts* – you must look out for the *nine of Hearts*, which will become your "Dream Card". When it appears (**2**) you call out . . .

"Stop!"

Reach out and take the nine of Hearts (**3**). Place it face downwards on the table without showing its face (**4**). Because she has been passing the cards singularly

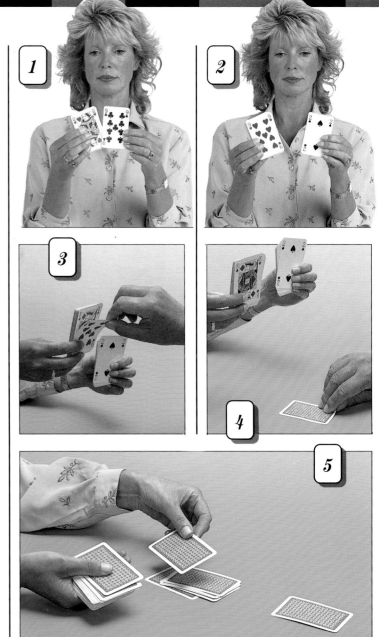

from hand to hand, the order of the pack has been reversed and the nine of Clubs and Queen of Hearts are now the top and second card from the top respectively.

> **"Let's see if you can find out what my dream card is without looking at it! Start dealing the cards *one at a time* onto the table in a pile . . . stop whenever you get the urge to."**

Suzy will deal the cards as instructed and will stop after a while (**5**). Our two "key" cards are now on the bottom of this pile.

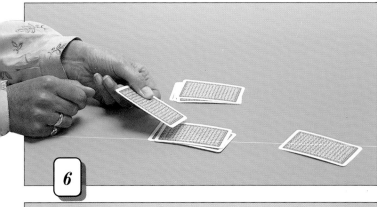

6

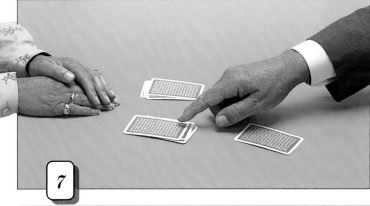

7

8

9

"Pick up the cards that you have dealt, Suzy. Deal them evenly, one at a time, into two piles. One of the piles will represent the value of my Dream Card and the other will represent its suit!"

Notice where the very last card goes (6)! Point to that pile (**7**).

"This pile will represent the value of my Dream Card – and the other pile the suit. Please turn the top card of each pile face up."

The first card that she turns over is the nine of Clubs (**8**).

"This is the value pile – so you say that my Dream Card is a *nine*. Right . . . Now turn over the top card on the suit pile."

She turns over the Queen of Hearts (**9**).

". . . and the 'suit' is Hearts. So you reckon that my dream card is the nine of Hearts! Turn it over and see if you are right.

She turns over your Dream Card (**10**). It *is* the nine of Hearts! Because it is self-working, the Dream Card Trick works like a dream every time!

10

➤ AFTERTHOUGHTS ◄

If the first two cards that she shows you are of the same suit, just ask her to give the cards another shuffle. If, after that, you still get two like-suited cards, get her to cut the cards. The odds of the first two cards still being of the same suit after all this are *extremely* remote.

OUT OF THIS WORLD

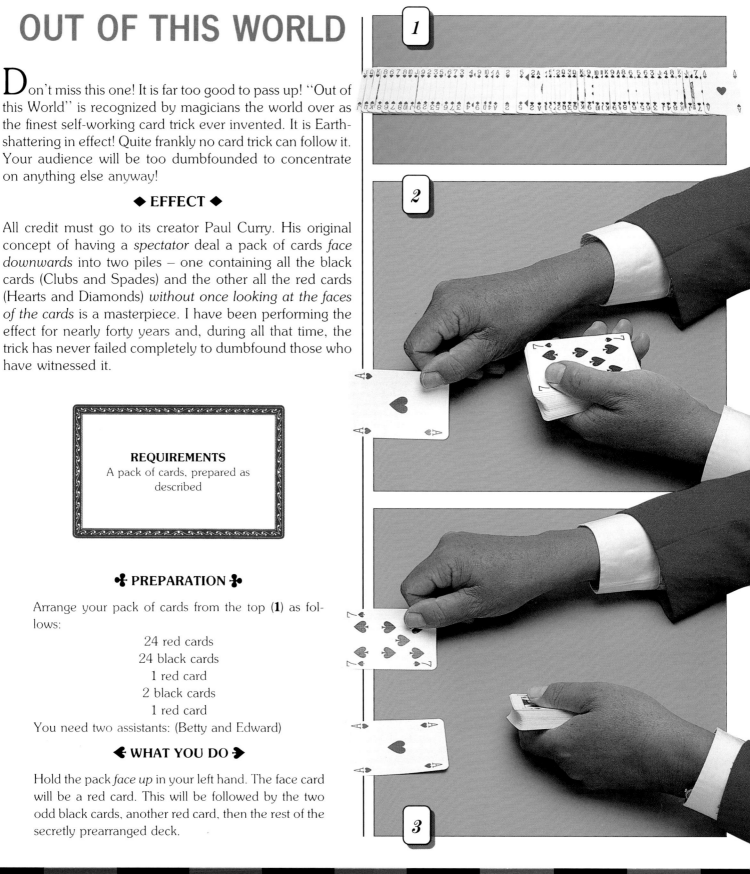

Don't miss this one! It is far too good to pass up! "Out of this World" is recognized by magicians the world over as the finest self-working card trick ever invented. It is Earth-shattering in effect! Quite frankly no card trick can follow it. Your audience will be too dumbfounded to concentrate on anything else anyway!

◆ EFFECT ◆

All credit must go to its creator Paul Curry. His original concept of having a *spectator* deal a pack of cards *face downwards* into two piles – one containing all the black cards (Clubs and Spades) and the other all the red cards (Hearts and Diamonds) *without once looking at the faces of the cards* is a masterpiece. I have been performing the effect for nearly forty years and, during all that time, the trick has never failed completely to dumbfound those who have witnessed it.

REQUIREMENTS
A pack of cards, prepared as described

♣ PREPARATION ♣

Arrange your pack of cards from the top (**1**) as follows:

> 24 red cards
> 24 black cards
> 1 red card
> 2 black cards
> 1 red card

You need two assistants: (Betty and Edward)

❰ WHAT YOU DO ❱

Hold the pack *face up* in your left hand. The face card will be a red card. This will be followed by the two odd black cards, another red card, then the rest of the secretly prearranged deck.

90

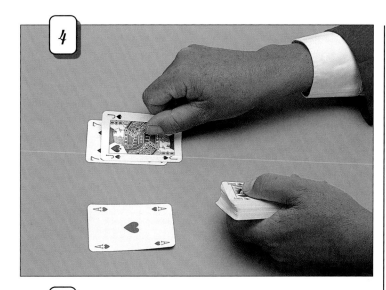

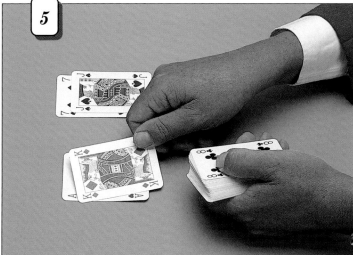

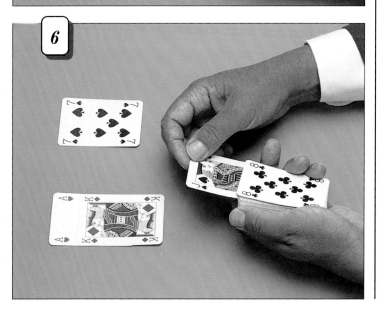

"If I were to ask you to take the pack and deal the cards into two separate piles – one pile containing all the red cards and the other containing all of the black cards – you would have no difficulty at all . . . because you have learned to tell red from black!"

As you are saying this, and by way of demonstration, you deal the top red card onto the table to the left (**2**), the next two black cards onto the table to your right (**3, 4**), slightly overlapping each other – then the next red card to the left on top of and slightly overlapping the red card (**5**).

"Well, that is exactly what I want you to do. The only difference is that I do not want you to look at the *faces* of the cards – *only the backs!"*

Pick up one of the two black cards that you have dealt and casually stick it back somewhere in the *top half* of the face-up pack (**6**) – then pick up one of the two red cards and slide it back somewhere in the *bottom half* of the pack (**7**). The pack is now arranged with 25 red cards followed by 25 black cards.

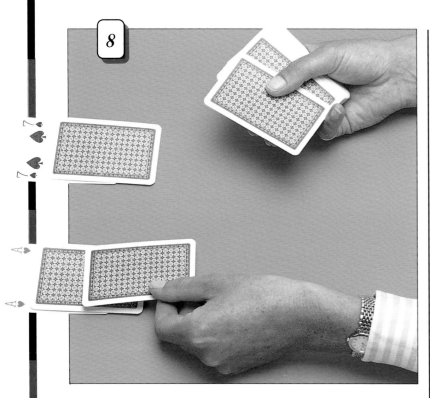

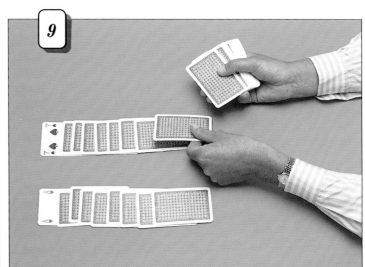

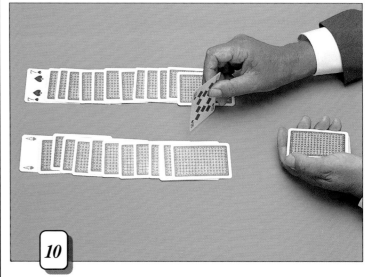

"I have left a red and a black card out to act as 'markers'. Take the pack from me. Keep it face down. I want you to start to deal the cards, one at a time, face downwards onto the two markers. If you think that the card that you are about to deal is a red one, deal it onto the left hand pile beneath the red marker. If, however, you think that it is a black card, deal it to the right beneath the black marker. Deal them one at a time and please don't go too fast because I have to keep up with you in my mind!"

Betty takes the cards and starts to deal them out haphazardly beneath the two markers (**8, 9**). As she does this, you must secretly count the cards. *Stop her as she deals the 24th card.*

Take back the rest of the pack from Betty. The top card will be a red one, followed by 25 black cards. Give the cards a little shuffle.

"Let's give Edward a try!"

Look through the cards without letting anyone else see their faces. Locate and remove the single red card (**10**) and lay it *face up* overlapping the last card that Betty dealt in the right hand (black) pile (**11**).

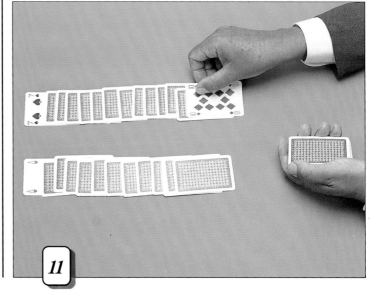

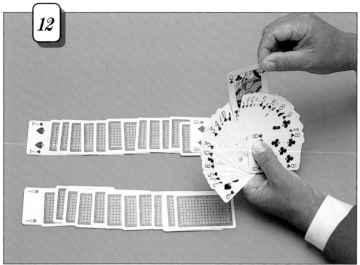

"We will change the markers over so that we can see where Betty left off and Edward begins. Let's find a black card as well"

Sort through the cards again as if searching for a black one! Finally remove one (**12**) and place *face up* on top of the last card in the left (red) pile (**13**). Give the balance of the cards to Edward and have him distribute them between the two piles, dealing them one at a time in any order he wishes (**14, 15**). This time you do not have to count. After he has dealt about a dozen cards, wait until he deals one beneath *his* red marker, the right hand pile. Shout out . . .

"Stop!"

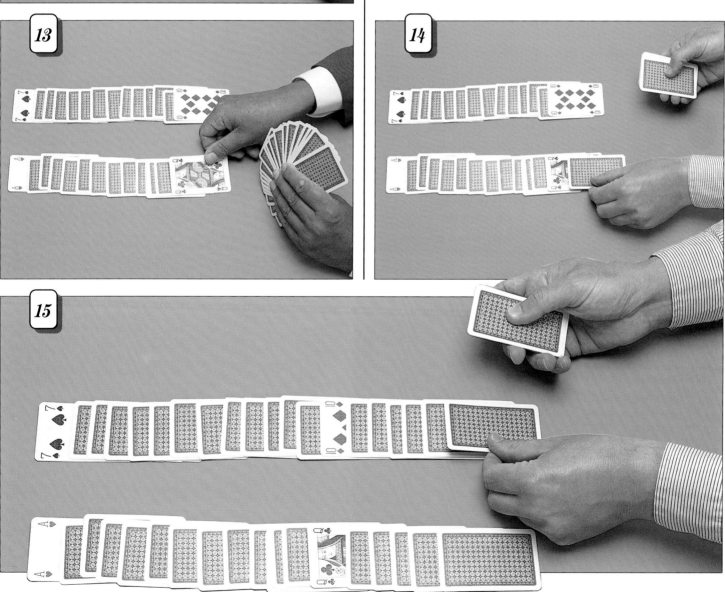

Pick up the card that he has just dealt (**16**) – turn it face up showing that it is black card (**17**) – then transfer it face down onto the other pile beneath the black marker (**18, 19**)!

"That one was wrong. But don't worry – you are doing very well!"

This little "subtlety" is most effective. Now have Edward finish the distribution of the remaining cards (**20**). The situation now is that the *left* pile is in the correct order with all face-down red cards beneath the red marker and all face-down black cards beneath the black marker. The *right* hand pile, however, is wrong. Black cards are at present beneath the red marker and red cards beneath the black marker. A minor problem for you, the Wonder Worker!

Scoop up all the cards in the right hand pile *except for the top black marker* (**21, 22**). Square the cards up and hold them in full view in your left hand (**23**).

"Let's just recap what has happened so far. Firstly the pack was shuffled. Secondly, it would not really matter if the pack was in a prearranged order because you both decided where each card should go. Is that right! Thirdly even if the cards were secretly marked on their backs, it would not make the slightest difference to the trick because, once more, *you* dealt the cards yourself. That's right, isn't it? How then do you explain this?"

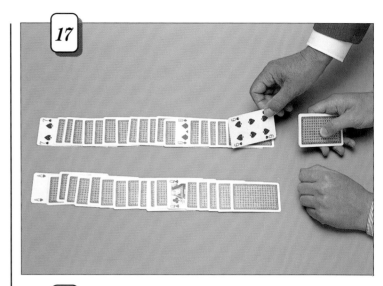

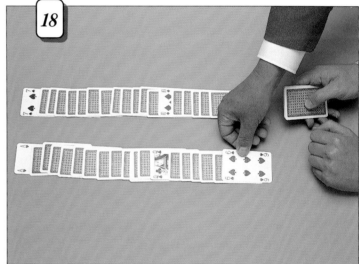

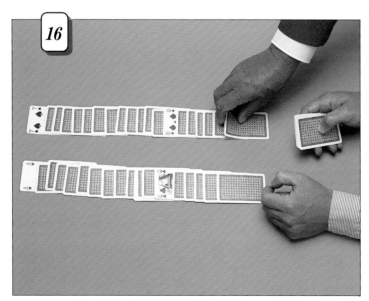

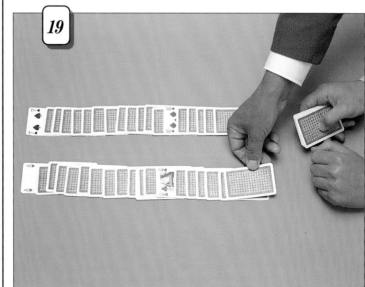

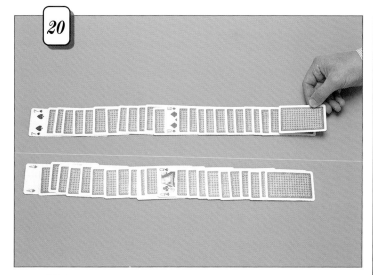

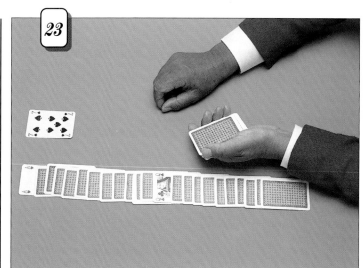

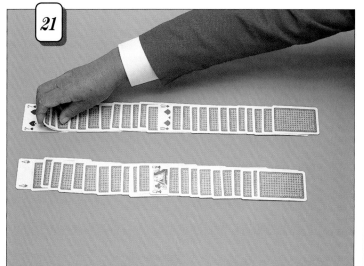

By setting the scene in this way you divert the spectators' concentration so that you can now get away with
the following extremely bold move.

Thumb off the top face-down cards into your right
hand (**24**) (just stop when you reach the face-up red
marker)!

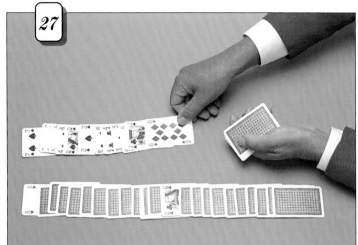

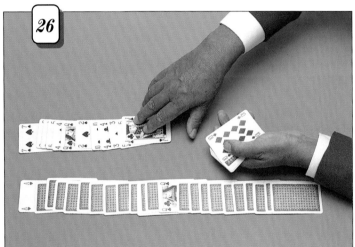

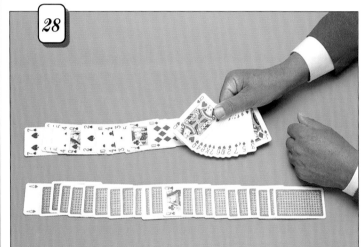

Turn them face up (**25**) and spread them out beneath the black marker that you left on the table (**26**). All the cards are black!

". . . all these cards are black . . ."

The *red* marker is now on top. Take it off and place it face up on the table (**27**). This leaves you with a pile of *red* cards in your left hand. Turn them face upwards and spread them out beneath the red marker (**28**).

". . . and all these are red! Now for the cards in the other pile? Let's see how successful you have been!"

Turn over the cards in the left hand line and show that they have in fact done the impossible! All the black cards are beneath the black marker (**29-31**) and all the red ones beneath the red marker (**32, 33**)!

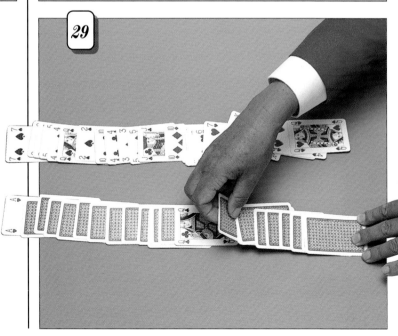

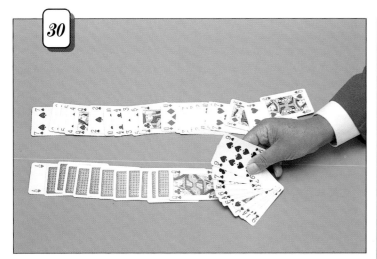

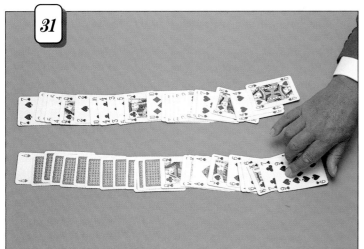

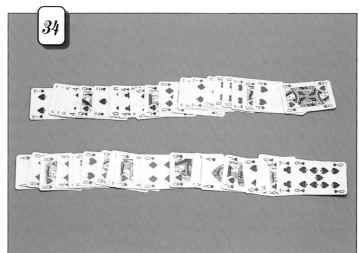

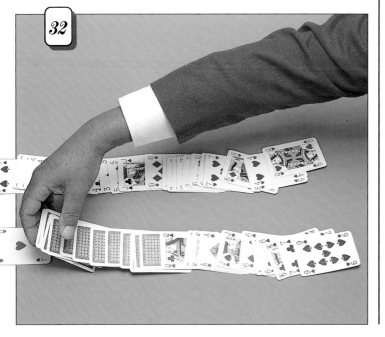

They have successfully colour-separated the entire pack without looking at the face of a single card (**34**)!

♣ AFTERTHOUGHTS ♣

1. Make sure that the dealers keep the cards low while dealing so they do not inadvertently "flash" the faces of the cards to the other spectators.

2. In my opinion, it is a mistake to be too perfect in an "mental" effect of this type. The trick can be greatly enhanced by making a couple of small errors. I usually prepare the original set-up by burying one black card among the red half and a couple of red cards among the black so that they will eventually be dealt out incorrectly. The psychology here is that if *all* the cards are separated perfectly it *must* be a trick. If, however, just a few of the cards are wrongly placed, there must be something in this mind-reading business after all!

RED OR BLACK

At the finish of the previous trick you are ideally placed to perform the following "quicky".

◆ EFFECT ◆

The pack is thoroughly shuffled and then spread out, face downwards, all over the table. The spectator (George) helps you do this. He now slides any card out of the jumbled spread and keeps his finger on it. You now do the same. You both turn your cards over – they are both the same colour! George selects another one – so do you. They are turned over and once again they are of the same colour. You both choose again. Again they are the same colour. A dozen times he chooses and a dozen times you match him colour for colour!

REQUIREMENTS
A pack of cards, prepared as described.

➤ PREPARATION ◄

When you gather the cards up, after performing "Out of this World", pick all the *red* cards up first. Secretly give them all a slight *upward* bend from end to end (**1**). Pick all the black cards up and give them a slight end-to-end *downward* bend (**2**).

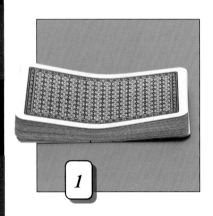

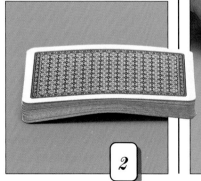

◄ WHAT YOU DO ➤

Now overhand shuffle the two halves together until the colours are well mixed. If you do a loose shuffle the cards will retain the "bends". Spread the cards out over the table surface and invite a spectator to help (**3**). Tell him that you want them really mixed up so that you can have no idea which is which or what is what!

"Now George . . . raise your index finger in the air and then bring it down to rest on the back of any card that you wish."

He does this.

"Pull it out of the spread towards you, but don't turn it over just yet."

By now you will have been able to detect which way George's card bends (**4**)! All you have to do is to look for one that bends in the same direction! After some apparent hesitation and concentration you drop your finger upon it and pull it out of the spread towards you (**5**).

4

5

6

7

8

9

"Turn your card face up, George."

When he has done that – you turn your card over too. If his is a red card so is yours (**6**)! If his is black – yours is black too (**7-12**)! Repeat this about a dozen times and then say . . .

". . . and so on and so on!"

. . .inferring that you can repeat the miracle "ad nauseam"!

✣ AFTERTHOUGHTS ✣

With a little practice you can make the bends (magicians call them crimps) very slight indeed! In fact you could really do away with one set of crimps completely – simply bend the red cards. Now, if the card has a bend it is a red one and if it has not got a bend, it is a black one!

This trick is deceptively simple. Do not insult the intelligence of your audience by drawing it out too long. A dozen selections is quite sufficient.

If you perform this trick immediately after doing "Out of this World", the spectators will assume that you are using your "mental powers" on this one too – especially if you perform it with a borrowed pack!

TIME GENTLEMEN PLEASE

This unusual trick is very "visual" and will create quite an impression. You will be accredited with superior mental powers by anyone who witnesses it.

◆ EFFECT ◆

A spectator (Vicky) thinks of a number. You successfully tell her what number she is thinking of and also predict which card she will choose long before she makes her choice!

REQUIREMENTS
A pack of cards
A sheet of paper
A pen

➤ PREPARATION ◄

Decide upon a card to use. Any one will do but, for the sake of our explanation, we will assume it to be the three of Clubs. Mark the back of the card with a light pencil dot in the white margin at the top left and bottom right corners (**1**). Put this marked three of Clubs *thirteenth* from the top and put the pack back in its case. On one side of the paper boldly write:

You will choose the three of Clubs

♣ WHAT YOU DO ♣

The spectators should *not* be aware of your prediction at this point, so place the paper (message side down) on the table. Put the card case near it and also have the pen nearby.

Take the paper and draw a large circle on it (**2**) and then fill in the numbers from one to twelve around the edge like a clock face. Put a bold dot in the centre (**3**). Turn to Vicky as you remove the cards from the case.

"This is a clock face, Vicky. Around it are twelve numbers. In a moment I will turn my back on you – if you will forgive my bad manners. While my back is turned, I want you to think of any one of the twelve numbers."

Hand her the pack of cards (**4**).

"When you have thought of the number, I want you to remove the same number of cards from the top of the pack and, without looking at them, I want you to sit on them!"

100

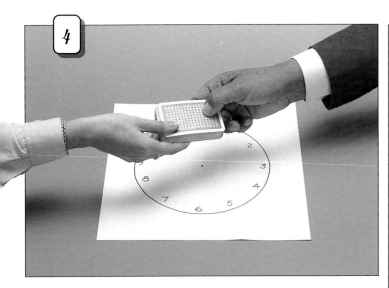

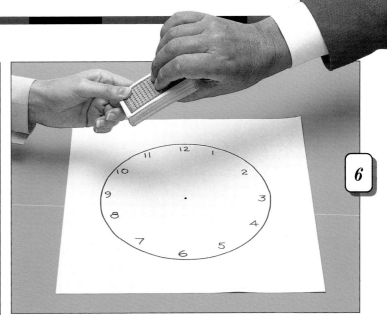

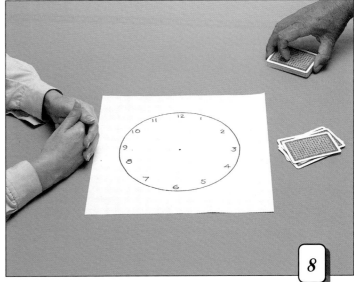

For example, if you thought of "three" – you would just remove three cards from the top of the pack and sit on them! Right?"

Turn your back so that you are obviously unable to see what she is doing. She does your bidding (**5**) and you turn to face her again when you are sure that she has completed the task. Take back the pack (**6**).

"We have twelve numbers."

Deal twelve cards from the top of the pack one at a time onto a little pile on the table (**7**), counting them out aloud as you do so. This action reverses the order of the twelve cards and, as you will realize later, is the reason the trick works. Put the rest of the pack to one side (**8**) and pick up the block of twelve cards.

Deal them out alongside the twelve written numbers on the clock starting at 1 o'clock with the first card (**9**), 2 o'clock with the second and so on until all twelve cards are in place (**10, 11**).

Watch for your secret pencil dot. Your marked card will now be indicating the number she was thinking of! It could actually be dealt in any one of the twelve positions but to assist a clear explanation of the trick we will assume that it has dropped on position number *seven*. Pick up the pen and place the point on the centre dot of the clock face circle.

"Vicky, I want you to think of your number. Don't call it out. Just think of it."

Slowly start to draw in a clock hand pointing directly at the number 7 (**12**). At the same time, say

"I think that you are thinking of the number 7! Am I right?"

In utter amazement she confirms this to be true! Have her remove the cards that she is sitting on. There are, indeed, seven cards (**13**)! Reach over and turn over the card in position 7. It is the three of Clubs (**14**). Clear away all the other cards (**15**).

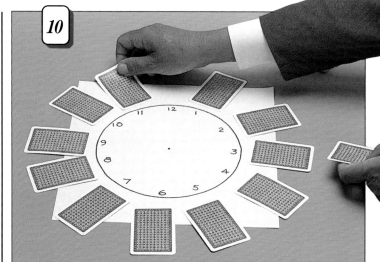

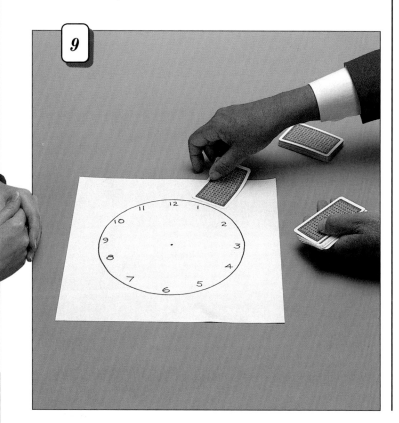

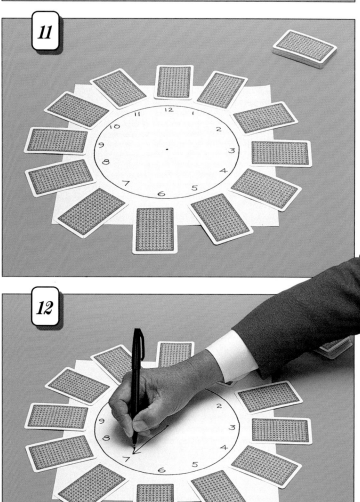

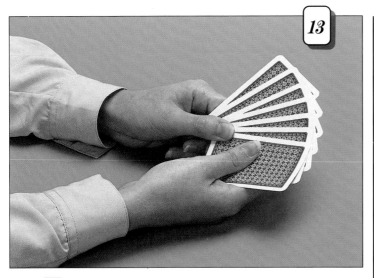

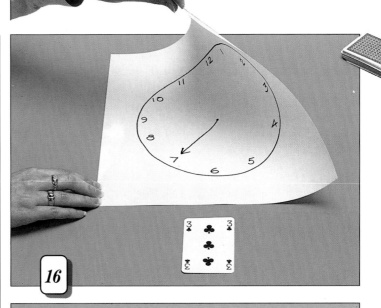

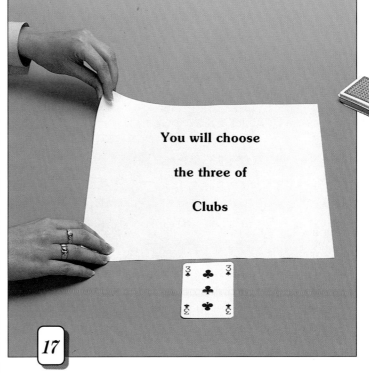

You will choose

the three of

Clubs

"The card that you have chosen is the three of Clubs. Now let me show you something really strange! Before we started I wrote you a message. That message is under the clock. Please pick up the clock. Turn it over and read what I wrote!"

She does as you say (**16, 17**). I think that you will agree that this is a mindboggling finish to a really smashing trick!

THE IMPOSSIBLE CARD TRICK

This is my favourite self-working card trick. It really looks "impossible".

◀ EFFECT ▶

A spectator chooses a card in a scrupulously fair manner. You can have no idea what it is. The card is returned by the spectator and the pack cut by her as many times as she wishes. Even under these test conditions you are able to find the chosen card!

REQUIREMENTS
A pack of cards, one of which is secretly marked

♣ PREPARATION ♣

In the last trick we made use of a card that had been secretly marked on its back in the top left and bottom right hand corners. We are going to use the card again but this time as a "locator" card or, as we magicians call it, a "key card." It will not tell us *what* the chosen card is. However, it will tell us *where* the chosen card is, which in this trick serves just as well! Position the key card so that it is the 26th card from the top (**1**). Place all the cards back in the case.

➤ WHAT YOU DO ◀

Remove the cards from the case and place them face downwards in front of the spectator (Lucy).

"Lucy, I want you to lift off about two thirds of the pack (over half) and place them here . . ."

Point to a position to the left of the pack. When she has done that (**2, 3**), point to second pile.

". . . and cut this pile roughly in half and place the cards here . . ."

Point to a position slightly further to the left. She does as you say (**4**). Your key card (the 26th card) is now somewhere in the centre of the middle pile. Point to the left hand pile again (**5**).

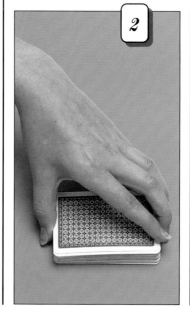

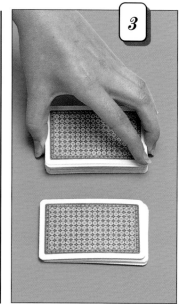

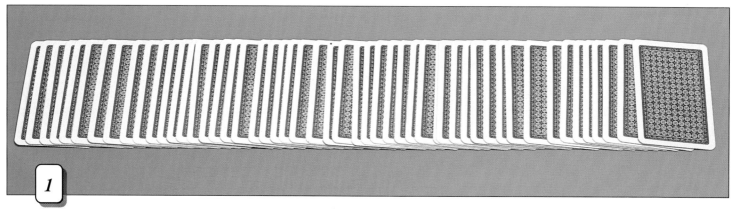

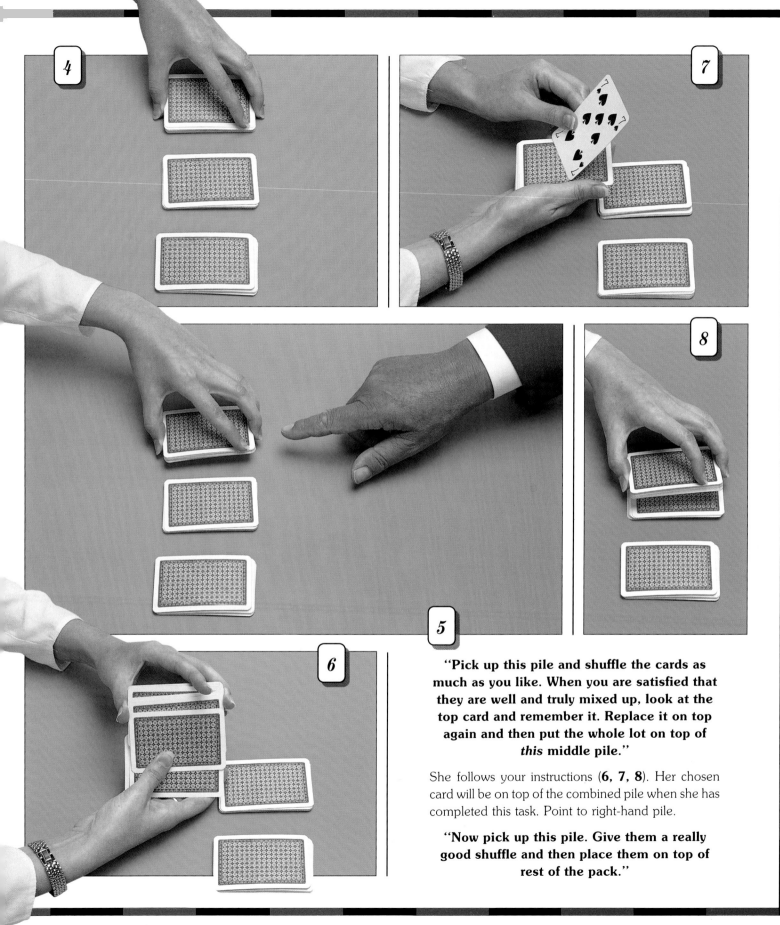

"Pick up this pile and shuffle the cards as much as you like. When you are satisfied that they are well and truly mixed up, look at the top card and remember it. Replace it on top again and then put the whole lot on top of *this* middle pile."

She follows your instructions (**6, 7, 8**). Her chosen card will be on top of the combined pile when she has completed this task. Point to right-hand pile.

"Now pick up this pile. Give them a really good shuffle and then place them on top of rest of the pack."

Again, Lucy does as she is told (**9, 10, 11**). *She can now give the pack as many complete cuts as she wishes.*

"So far I haven't touched the cards at all. You have shuffled them – chosen one – shuffled again and then repeatedly cut the cards. It is quite impossible for me to know the name of your card."

Lucy has to agree because everything that you have just said is absolutely true! Now take the cards and spread them out face downwards on the table in a line from left to right (**12**). Make sure that no two cards stick together and that the *edge of every card can be seen.*

"Hold my right wrist, Lucy. I am going to attempt to receive impulses from you and find your chosen card."

Extend your index finger and, starting from the *left* hand side (**13**), begin to move it slowly along the line of cards and about 5cm above them (**14**). When you sight the pencil dotted corner (your key card) count this as number 1, and continue to count the cards *silently* to yourself until you have reached 26. This will be the chosen card! Do not pick it out right away though. Go a little past it. Hover over the cards in the vicinity as though you are beginning to receive an "impulse" from the cards. Then go back to the 26th card (**15**) and pull it clear of the spread, still face down (**16**).

"What card did you choose, Lucy?"

"The seven of Spades." Slowly turn the face-down card over to show that your "impulse" was correct (**17**)! The *impossible* has been achieved!

➤ AFTERTHOUGHTS ◀

If you reach the end of the line (the right-hand end) before you have reached the count of 26, merely continue the count back at the left-hand end. The chosen card will always be 26 away from your key card.

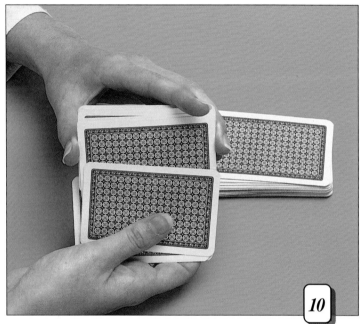

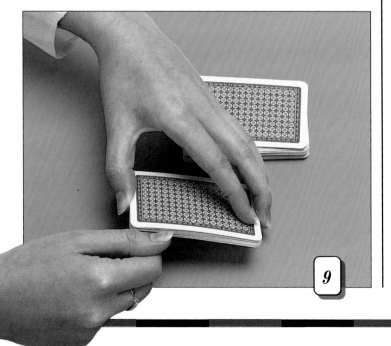

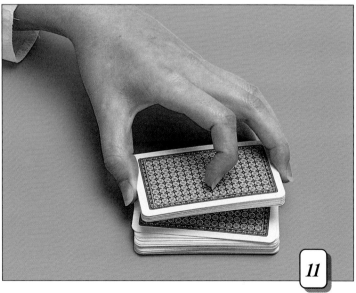

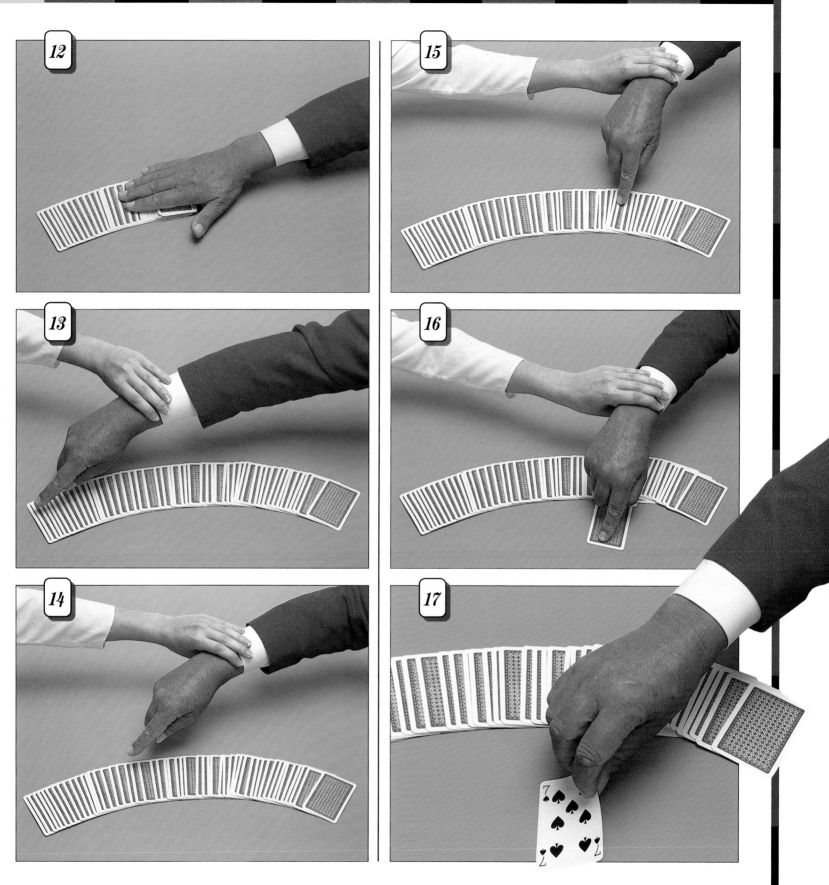

THE CIRCUS CARD TRICK

This is an old fairground "con" trick, often used to fleece the unwary!

◄ EFFECT ►

When you attempt to find a spectator's chosen card, she is convinced that you have made a mistake. Convinced enough to bet all her money on it! You turn the tables on her in a very funny way.

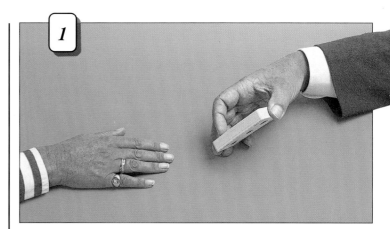

> **REQUIREMENTS**
> A pack of cards

◆ WHAT YOU DO ◆

Let us call your friend Mary. Get her to shuffle the cards. As you take them back, secretly look at the bottom card and remember it (**1**). Do not make a big thing of this – just be casual. This card will be your key to finding the card that Mary is about to choose. We will assume that your *key card* is the three of Hearts, although it could be any card. Spread the cards out and get Mary to choose any card she likes (**2**). If there is anybody else watching she should also show it to them, because if she forgets the name of her card you will feel very foolish too!

Ask her to put her card back on *top* of the pack (**3**) and then cut the cards so that her chosen card is buried somewhere in the middle (**4, 5**). This puts your key card (the three of Hearts) right on top of it! Get her to cut the pack and complete the cut once or twice more, and, if anyone else is watching, let them have a cut too. *Just make sure each time that they merely cut off the top half and then put what was the bottom half on top of it.* Do not let the two important cards get separated. Your key card will still be right on top of her chosen card even after all these cuts.

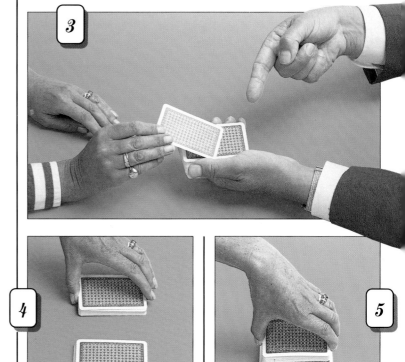

Tell Mary that you can read with your finger tips! You will be able to find her card without looking, by just feeling the raised patterns left by the printer's ink!

Hold the pack face down and start to deal the cards *face up*, one at a time, onto the table (**6**). In doing this, pretend that you are feeling the ink on each one before you turn it upwards. Keep doing this until you spot your key card (3H) (**7**). *The next card that you turn over will be Mary's chosen one!* Take it off just like the others, feel its face and deal it face up too. We will assume that it is the four of Clubs (**8**).

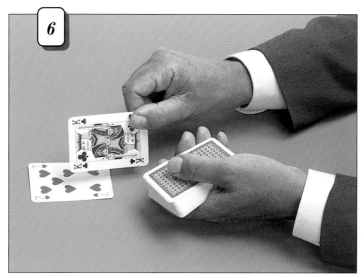

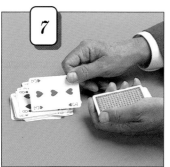

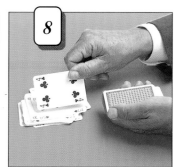

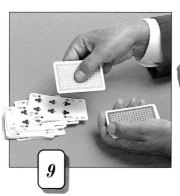

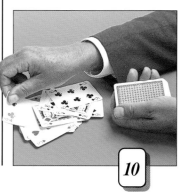

Do not let on that you know that it is her chosen one at this point. Keep a straight face and continue feeling and turning over another five or six cards. Now you must really act! Push off the next card (**9**). Feel it. Feel it again. Smell it. Hold it up to your ear as if you are listening to it, then feel it yet again! What you now say is very important – so practise until you get it right.

"I bet you £10 that the very next card I turn over will be the one that you chose!"

Give the card that you are holding another feel. Do you see what we are doing? Mary is being led to believe that you are going to turn over the card that you are holding. She has already seen the four of Clubs pass by, so she will be very keen to accept your bet! As soon as she agrees to the bet you reach down to the pile of cards already dealt and turn the four of Clubs face down (**10, 11**). You have done exactly what you said you would do!

This trick was originally used by swindlers in circus fairgrounds years ago. That is how it got its name. We, however, are entertainers, not cheats, so you must refuse to take Mary's money.

➤ AFTERTHOUGHTS ◄

If Mary should want to take the bottom card when she makes her original choice, let her! Your planned key card now becomes Mary's chosen card and as we already know what it is, we can continue as described above and just wait for the three of Hearts to show itself. You can even let her give the pack a thorough shuffle!

THE FABULOUS FOUR

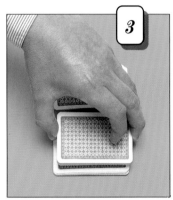

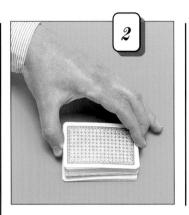

Unlike "The Acrobatic Aces", this version is completely self-working. The spectator does all the work for you.

◄ EFFECT ➤

You do not touch the cards yourself. In this fabulous self-working trick, the spectator does all the mixing and cutting and yet still manages magically to find the four Aces – all by himself!

> **REQUIREMENTS**
> A pack of cards, prepared as described

◆ PREPARATION ◆

Secretly place the four Aces face downwards on top of the pack (**1**). Place the pack on the table in front of the spectator and you are ready to begin.

♣ WHAT YOU DO ♣

Ask the spectator (James) to cut the pack into four more or less equally sized piles in a row by dropping off a section at a time (**2-5**). By doing this the original top section (with the Aces on top) end up in the fourth position (**6**).

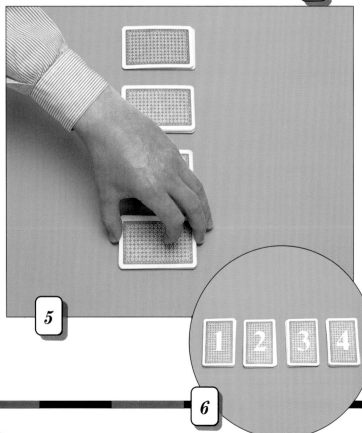

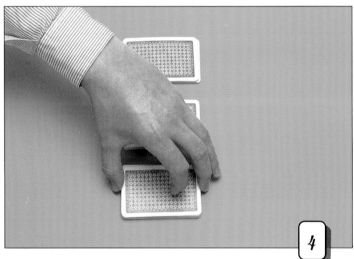

You have nothing to do now except tell James what to do – so please make your instructions to him very clear! You say,

"Pick up pile number one."

Point to it (**7**) so that there can be no mistake . . .

"Without looking at them, I want you to take three cards from the top of your little pile and put them at the bottom of your little pile. Now – also from the top of your pile – deal one card onto each of the other three piles."

When this has been done (**8-12**) . . .

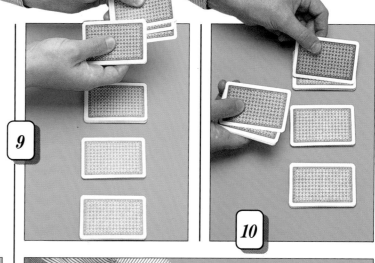

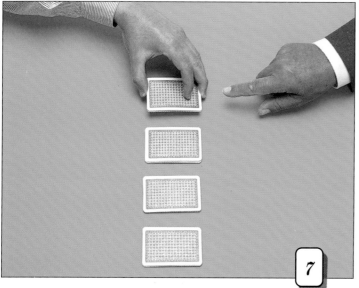

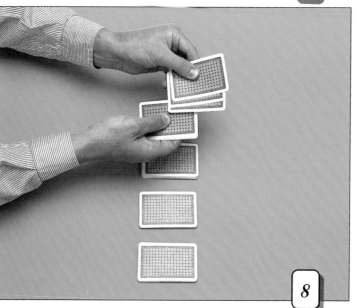

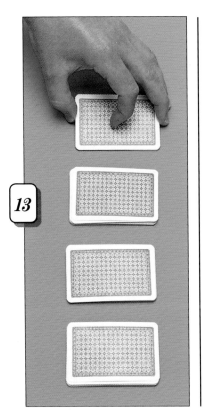

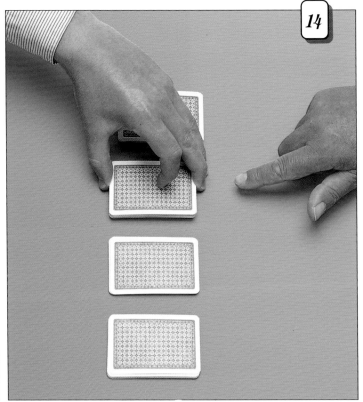

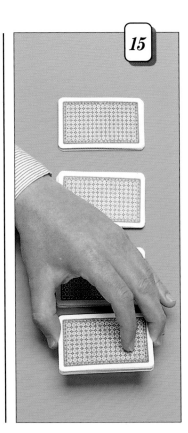

"**Put your pile back on the table again.**" He does so (**13**) . . . "**Pick up pile number two (14) – again transfer three cards from the top to the bottom and then one card onto each of the other three piles.**"

Have James do the same with the other two piles as well. You will notice that, when he gets to the last pile (**15**), the three cards that have been placed, one by one, on top of pile number *four* get transferred to the bottom by the spectator and then, unknown to him, he deals an Ace on the top of piles Nos. 1, 2 and 3 (**16**)! All four piles now have an Ace on top. Very sneaky!!

"**You did all the cutting, shuffling about and moving of the cards yourself. Is that true?**"

James has to agree that this is so.

"**I call this trick 'The Fabulous Four'. Do you know why? Please turn up the top card on each pile!**"

Bingo! The four Aces now stare him in the face (**17-20**), and he did it all by himself. (Well – almost)!

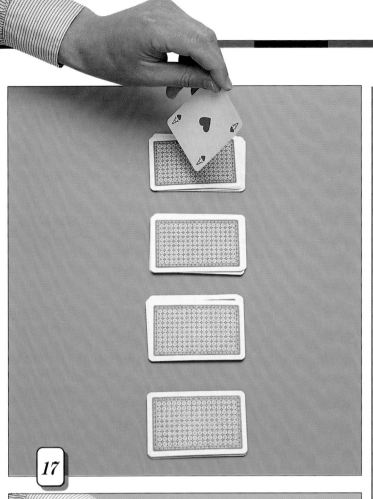

17

18

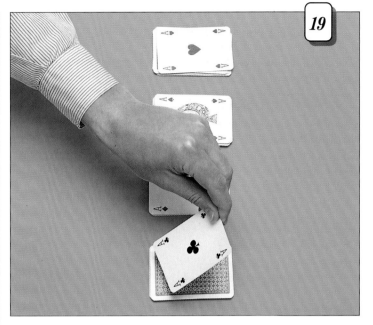

19

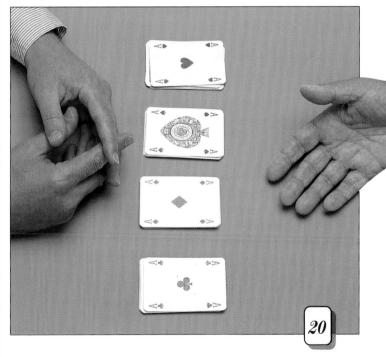

20

♣ AFTERTHOUGHTS ♣

The cutting – transferring – and dealing of the cards is cleverly designed to confuse the spectator so that he will be unable to remember the exact sequence of his duties. James will think that he just shuffled and then cut to the four Aces. A false shuffle (retaining the four Aces on top) at the beginning, *before* you place the pack of cards on the table, will enhance the overall effect.

A MATHEMATICAL CERTAINTY

For downright subtlety this classic takes some beating. The trick is a very good one and the misdirection – fabulous!

◆ EFFECT ◆

You correctly name the cards that a spectator hides in his pocket under what appear to be impossible conditions. This brief description does not do justice to this strong effect, so read on!

```
REQUIREMENTS
A pack of cards
```

➤ PREPARATION ◄

You must know and remember the names of the third and fourth cards from the *bottom* of the pack. If you make the third one the three of Hearts and the fourth one the four of Spades while you practise, you will find them easier to remember (**1**). Once you get the hang of it, you should in fact use whatever cards you happen to find in those positions.

♣ WHAT YOU DO ♣

We will call our spectator Paul.

"Cut the pack into two piles and then touch one."

You do not ask him to *choose* one pile but merely *touch* one (**2**). This is most important because you must get the spectator to take the original bottom half of the pack, seemingly of his own free will. If he touches it, get him to pick it up while you pick up the other half (**3**). If, however, he touches the original top half of the pack, pick it up yourself and say,

"Thank you. You take the other half, Paul."

Cheeky, isn't it! This type of force is called *Equivoque*. Magicians regularly use such careful choice of words to achieve otherwise impossible results.

"I want you to duplicate everything that I do. Will you count your cards first?"

You count by dealing the cards one by one onto the table (**4**) thus reversing the order of the cards. The noted two cards will now be the third and fourth card from the top of his packet.

Announce the number of cards in your packet and then ask him how many he has. Behave as if the matter was important. This is just a valuable "misdirection". Whatever he announces, ask him to discard one card. *He will naturally discard the top one* (**5**).

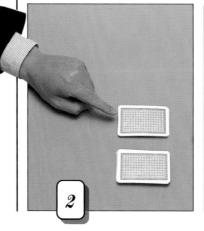

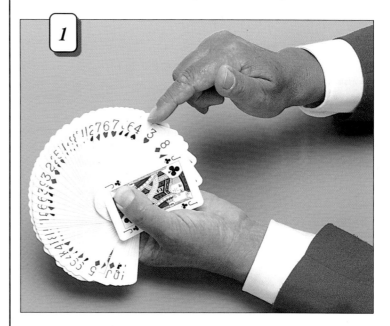

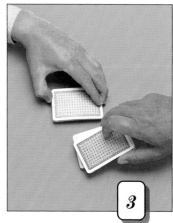

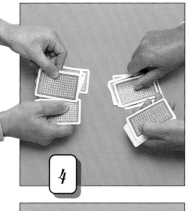

4

5

6

7

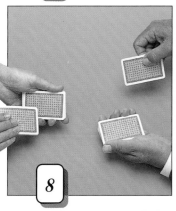

8

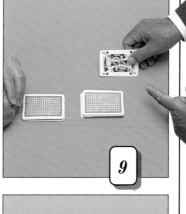

9

10

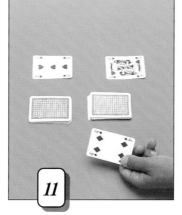

11

"Please continue doing what I do, Paul."

Take the top card of your pile and slip into the centre (**6**). Wait while he does the same. Take a card from the bottom and push it into the centre (**7**). Take another card from the top and put it into your *left* jacket pocket. Take another from the bottom and push it into the centre of cards that you hold. Take one more card from the top and put it into your *right* coat pocket (**8**). Replace your half of the pack on the table.

These actions have been deliberately designed to drag as many "red-herrings" across the trail as possible! If Paul has been duplicating your actions with his own half of the pack, the card in his left hand coat pocket was originally the *third* from the bottom (three of Hearts), and the one in his right was originally *fourth* (four of Spades).

You bring the trick to a climax by saying . . .

"It is a mathematical certainty that this card in my right hand pocket being the . . ." You bring it out and name it as you show it (**9**) . . . "The card in your *left* hand pocket is the three of Hearts!"

You name the first of the two cards that you remembered. And you are right (**10**)!

"And this one being the . . ." Remove the card from your other pocket and name it as you show it (**11**) . . . "The one in your other pocket will be the four of Spades!"

Name the second card that you remembered (**12**).

"Am I right?"

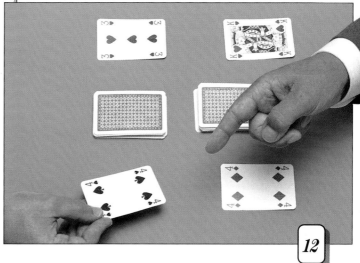

12

7-UP!

This trick really packs a punch, and builds up to an excellent climax. I am sure you will have fun with it.

❧ EFFECT ❧

The spectator finds the four sevens in a startling and amazing manner. They appear, one at a time, and each appearance is more startling than the last.

REQUIREMENTS
A pack of cards, prepared as described

◆ PREPARATION ◆

Place two of the sevens on the top of the pack, one seven on the bottom and then turn the last seven face up and insert it, still reversed, about two thirds of the way down (**1**).

♣ WHAT YOU DO ♣

Hold the pack in your left hand in the dealing position. Take care not to "flash" the bottom seven. This time we will call your assistant Penny.

"Penny . . will you call out a number between 5 and 10 please."

It is a psychological fact that 80 per cent of the time people will say "seven" when asked to call out a number under ten. We will assume that Penny is no exception. The Afterthoughts section at the end of this trick's explanation will tell you how to continue should she be one of the other 20 per cent. So Penny, obligingly says . . . "Seven".

Deal out seven cards into two rows as illustrated (**2**). The second card dealt (a seven) goes beneath the first card dealt (also a seven). The third card goes to the left of the first card, the fourth goes to right of the

second, the fifth to the right of the first, the sixth to the left of the second and the last card to the left of the top row. Sounds complicated? It's not really – just take another look at the illustration (**3**) and all will be made clear. You have a row of four cards beneath which is a row of three cards and the sevens are both second from the right. Right? Right! Put the rest of the pack to one side, face down.

"Oh dear! I really wanted an even number! But don't worry, we will see if I can do the trick with seven cards. There are two rows of cards in front of you and, in a moment, I will ask you to choose one of the two rows. However, we need a row with four cards in it – so if you choose *this* row . . ."

Point to the row with just the three cards in it . . .

"We will just have to slide the last card that I dealt downwards to make a row of four. O.K.?"

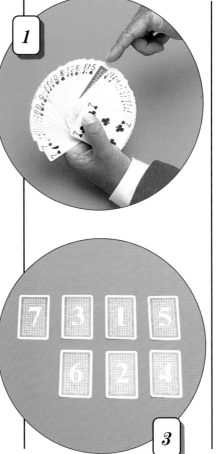

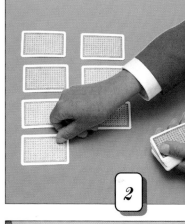

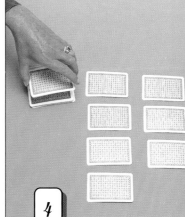

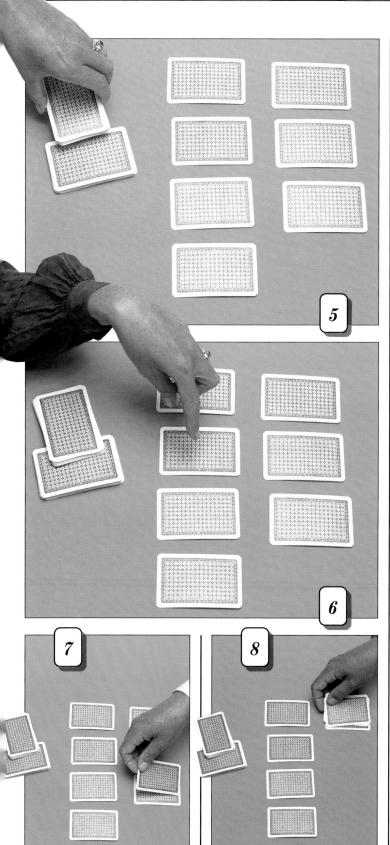

Slide the last card downwards, and then back up again to its original place.

"Before you choose your row, I want you to cut the pack for me."

She cuts off about half of the pack. Ask her to pick up the bottom half and rest it across the cut-off section (**4, 5**). Of course, the original bottom seven is the bottom card of the upper half of the cut pack. Now bring her attention back to the two rows of cards.

"All right, now point to a row, Penny."

Once she has pointed to a row (**6**) and you have made sure that it has four cards in it, gather up the other three cards and place them, face down, on top of the upper section of the cross-cut pack (**7, 8, 9**). *In so doing, make sure that the centre card (the seven) ends up as the top card. This is very important.*

Penny is now looking at the row of four cards spread out before her. Your task is to get her to choose the second card from her left which we know is a seven. Be careful not to use the word "choose". We are going to use the technique of *Equivoque* again, using a careful choice of vocabulary to create an inexplicable mystery. The seven is psychologically placed so that 70 per cent of the time it will be her first choice. Say

"I want you to point to one of these four cards."

If she points to the seven (**10**) – Bingo!

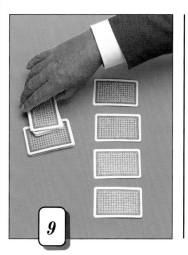

You need worry no more. Just ask her to turn it over (**11**) and then continue with the conclusion of the trick explained below. If, however, she points to one of the other three cards – say:

". . . and point to another one, too."

If she points to our Secret Seven this time, take the *other two cards away and discard them* leaving her two selections on the table.

"Place a finger on the back of each card, please . . . now lift up one of your fingers."

If she lifts her finger off the other indifferent card, take it away and discard it. You are home and dry again because her finger still rests upon the back of the seven. If she lifts her finger off the seven, say,

"Are you sure? O.K.!"

Push the seven closer to her – remove the other card from beneath her other finger and discard it! The other scenario is that her first two selections do *not* include the Secret Seven. In that case you just remove and discard the two cards and then proceed with the remaining two exactly as described above. You just cannot lose! Your "technical" work is almost complete. From now on it is *presentation* all the way. Well, almost!

"Penny, I want to show you a very remarkable thing. I asked you to call out a number. You said 'seven'. We dealt out seven cards and you chose one of them. Please turn it over!" She does (**12**). **"Your chosen card is a *seven*!"**

Lift up the top half of the cross-cut pack (**13**) and show the card at its face (the original bottom card)!

"You have cut the pack at a *seven*!"

Remove the seven and place it face up next to the one that is already there (**14**). Replace the rest of the cards squarely on top of the remainder of the pack (**15**) and then spread them evenly across the table to reveal the one *reversed* card (**16**)!

"The only reversed card in the pack is a *seven*!"

Gather up all the cards after removing the face-up seven, which goes down with the other two (**17**). The top card is now the remaining Secret Seven!

"That just leaves one seven to find! *Watch*!"

You are now going to drop the pack onto the table and the final seven is going to flip itself over and come to rest face up on the deck! You will have to practise this a few times before you get the hang of it. Believe me the practice will be well worth it because it is a very snappy way to reveal a chosen card!

Hold the pack in your right hand, fingers at the top short edge, thumb at the bottom short edge. Push the top card over with your left thumb, so that it projects over the long edge of the pack by about 2cm (**18**). The back of your right hand prevents this from being obvious to the spectator. Hold the pack about 25cm above the table top and drop the pack with a *very slight* downward thrust. This downward thrust will act against the air pressure and the projecting card will flip face upwards (**19**)! Keep practising until you get the "feel" for this. It is a very startling revelation and a great climax to this entertaining trick!

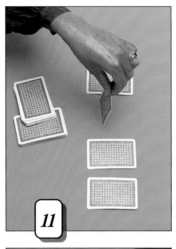

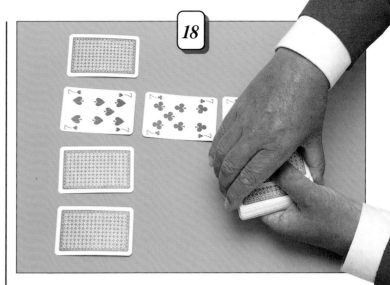

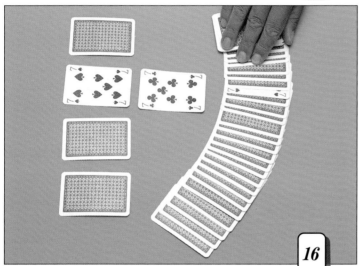

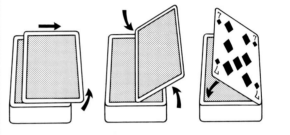

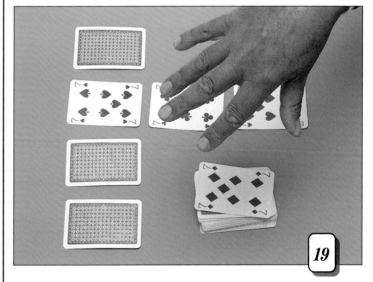

➤ AFTERTHOUGHTS ◄

If the number "seven" is not chosen, do not worry – just deal out the number of cards that the spectator nominates, keeping track of the two Secret Sevens, and then carry on as described. In your "winding up" speech you simply ignore her number as if it has no bearing on the trick. Just emphasize the appearance of the Mystic Sevens!

TOO HOT TO HANDLE

Y ou will have great fun with this one! You achieve the impossible yet the method could not be simpler.

◀ EFFECT ▶

A spectator freely chooses a card from a shuffled pack and returns it to the centre of the pack. In an instant her chosen card becomes the only reversed card in the pack!

REQUIREMENTS
A pack of cards with backs that have white borders
An assistant. We will call her Anne

➤ WHAT YOU DO ◀

Hand the pack of cards to Anne and have her shuffle them. Take back the pack and spread them between your hands so that Anne can remove one (**1**).

"Look at the card that you have chosen and remember it please (2). In a moment I will ask you to put your card back into the pack and then I will place the cards behind my back so that I can no longer see the cards."

While you are saying this, apparently by way of demonstrating, you put the pack behind your back. *As soon as it is out of sight* turn the whole pack *face up* (**3**) and then turn the first two cards *face down* (**4**, **5**). This should take little more than a second to do. Bring the pack into view again. Keep the cards well squared up. Now, what looks like a face-down pack is, in fact, a face-up pack with just two cards face downward on the top!

"Push your card back into the pack, Anne — anywhere you wish."

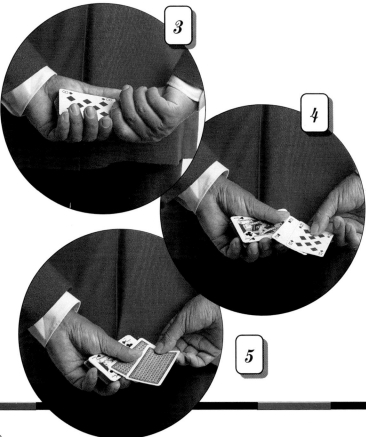

Anne does as you ask (**6**). Unknown to her she has returned her card to a face-up deck (apart from the couple of cards on the top)! Hold the pack firmly while she does this and the illusion will be perfect. Keep the pack fairly low so that she does not see the back of the bottom card.

"Because you have handled the card it should be slightly warmer than the rest! I will try to find your card with the aid of my very sensitive fingertips. It should feel 'red hot' to me!"

Put the pack behind your back. Once it is out of sight, turn the top two cards *face up again* (**7**, **8**)! Now her chosen card is the *only* reversed card in the pack! Flip the whole pack over (**9**) and bring it out again. Take your time over this. Pretend that you are having a bit of difficulty at first.

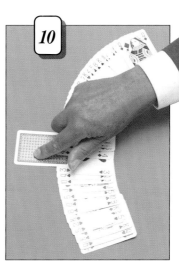

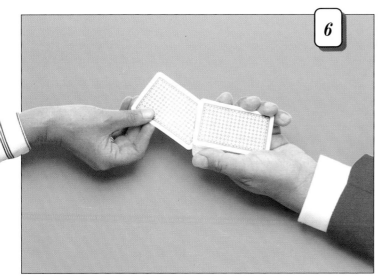

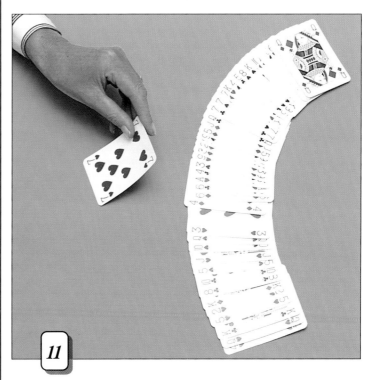

Spread the cards face upwards on the table in a sweep from left to right showing that there is one solitary face-down card in the pack. Push it slightly out of the spread (**10**).

"If I am right, this card will be the one that you chose. What was the name of your card, Anne?" Anne names her card.
"It's too hot for *me* to handle! Would *you* please turn the card over for me!"

She turns over the one reversed card (**11**). Q.E.D.!

DO AS I DO

Coincidence tricks are very popular with card magicians and this is one of the best.

♣ EFFECT ♣

Two packs of cards are used. The spectator selects a card from his pack – you remove one from yours. By an absolutely amazing coincidence, you both choose the same card!

REQUIREMENTS
Two unprepared packs of cards with different back designs

◆ WHAT YOU DO ◆

Put the two packs face down on the table side by side. Your assistant (Luke) stands on the other side of the table

"Now Luke, this trick is called 'Do As I Do'. I want you to try to duplicate my actions as closely as you can. Do everything that I do."

Pick up a pack of cards. Luke will pick up the other one. Give your cards a thorough shuffle. Luke will do his best (**1**)! While Luke is absorbed with his shuffling, secretly look at and remember the card that you have shuffled to the bottom of your own pack (**2**). This will be your 'key card'. Let us assume that it is the two of Spades.

"You have just shuffled your pack and I have shuffled mine. So it must be true that I don't know the order of your cards and it is certainly true that you don't know the order of mine. So you take my pack and I will take yours." You take his pack and he takes yours (**3**). **"Now reach somewhere into the middle of the pack – remove any card – remember it – then place it on top of the pack. I will do the same."**

You show him how by removing any card and looking at it. Pretend to remember it and then place it on top of the pack. You can forget the card that you have just seen because it will play no further part in our trick. Luke does as you do (**4, 5**) only, you hope, he will remember the name of the card that he has chosen! You had better ask him again to remember it because if he does not, it will ruin the trick!

"Now cut and complete the cut."

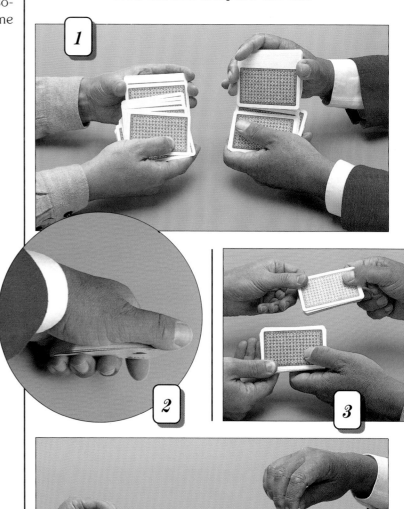

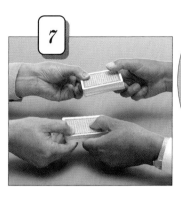

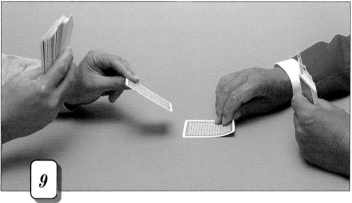

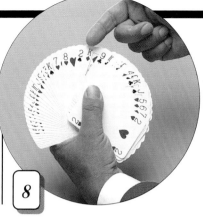

Show him how and in following your actions (**6**) he will unknowingly bring your "key card" to rest on top of his chosen card!

"Let's cut again . . ."

You both do another complete cut and then a third.

"Are you happy with that – or shall we cut again?"

Whatever he says, you oblige. Just make sure that each cut is a complete one that does not disturb the circular order of the cards. We do not want his chosen card and your remembered key card to be separated.

"Now that we have thoroughly mixed the cards, we will exchange packs again. You take mine – I'll take yours (7). Now this is want I want you to do. Look through the deck that you are holding and remove the card that you are thinking of and place it face downwards on the table – I'll look through this pack and remove the one that I am thinking of. Remember, this trick is called 'Do As I Do' so please let me remove my card first and place it on the table before you put down yours."

Thumb through the pack that you are now holding and search for "key card" (the two of Spades). The card next to and beneath it will be his chosen one (**8**)! Remove it and place it face downwards on the table without showing its face. Luke does the same (**9**). All you have got to do now is wind up the trick (and Luke)!

"Do you believe in coincidence, Luke? We both chose a pack of cards. We both shuffled, and cut, and thought of cards at random. You tried to duplicate my actions to the best of your ability. Wouldn't it be amazing then if we both thought of the same card? Turn them face upwards Luke (10)!"

FINAL AFTERTHOUGHTS

There are a few general do's and don'ts for a magician that I would briefly like to touch upon.

1. Don't overdo it! It is always a mistake to do too many tricks. Four or five knockout tricks should be quite enough for one session. Leave them wanting more.

2. Never divulge your secrets! If someone asks you ". . . how do you do it?" . . . just answer: "Very Well!" or "It's Magic!".

3. Never repeat a trick unless you can create the same effect by using a totally different method. Forewarned is forearmed – if an audience knows *what* is about to happen there is much more chance that they will discover *how* it happens.

4. People will be watching your hands so make sure that they are clean and well manicured.

5. Practise until you know the trick backwards – until you can perform it in your sleep. The more you practise the slicker you will become. Practise in front of a mirror so you can see how it looks from the spectator's point of view.

6. Know what you are going to say before you say it. Your patter has to be practised as much as your technique. There is nothing worse than a waffling magician. You could write yourself a script or record it on tape to help you develop a smooth flow.

7. These tricks are described and photographed from a **right-handed person's** point of view. If you are left-handed, just reverse the instructions.

8. Do not try to make your audience look foolish. Some people get annoyed if they cannot work out a trick. Explain beforehand that your object is to *entertain* them. If they knew how you did your tricks, it would not be worth doing them in the first place, would it?!

9. Tricks do sometimes go wrong. It happens to the best of us. Sometimes you will be able to disguise your embarrassment because you very seldom tell an audience what you are going to do until you have done it! If it is not possible, the best policy is to laugh it off and go on to your next trick. Try not to be thrown off your stride by the problem. Find out what went wrong and, at your first opportunity, get in some more practice so that you do not make the same mistake again.

10. Smile! Do not take your newly found skill as a wonderworker too seriously. You will not be entertaining if you do. Nobody likes a smart alec.

My sincere wish in writing these books is to encourage new talent, so if, after reading this book, you feel that you would like to progress further, the following notes will be most helpful.

MAGIC CLUBS AND SOCIETIES

Unlike other branches of the entertainment world, magicians seek one another's company and revel in the exchange of ideas. You would do well to join a club (most large towns have one). Space prevents me from mentioning all of them here. These are the main ones:

The Magic Circle
The Players Theatre
Villiers Street
The Strand
London
WC2 6NG

For details write to:
Christopher Pratt, Secretary of the Magic Circle, 13 Calder Avenue, Brookmans Park, Herts, AL9 7AH

International Brotherhood of Magicians
Headquarters
P.O. Box 192090
St. Louis,
MO 63119-9998
U.S.A.

The British Ring (No.25) of the International Brotherhood of Magicians can be contacted by writing to:
Jeffrey Atkins, The Hon. Secretary, The British Ring I.B.M., Kings Garn, Fritham Court, Fritham, Lyndhurst, Hants, SO43 7HH

British Magical Society
Headquarters
Birmingham and Midland Institute
Margaret Street
Birmingham
B3 3BS

For details write to:
Neil Roberts, Hon. Secretary, British Magical Society,
46 Selby Close, Yardley, Birmingham B26 2AR

The Society of American Magicians
Write to:
John Apperson
S.A.M. Membership Development
2812 Idaho
Granite City
Illinois 62040
U.S.A.

MAGIC MAGAZINES

These keep you up-to-date with the latest news from the world of magic and are essential reading for serious magicians.

Abracadabra (weekly)
Goodliffe Publications Ltd
150 New Road
Bromsgrove
Worcestershire
B60 2LG

Magic (monthly)
Stan Allen & Associates
7380 South Eastern Avenue
Suite 124-179
Las Vegas
NV 89123
U.S.A.

Genii (monthly)
P.O. Box 36068
Los Angeles
CA 90036
U.S.A.

MAGIC SUPPLIERS

There are many specialist shops around the world which supply the magical fraternity with apparatus and books that are not otherwise available. They all produce catalogues. I list a few below.

L. Davenport & Co
7 Charing Cross Underground Shopping Arcade
The Strand
London
WC2N 4HZ

International Magic Studio
89 Clerkenwell Road
Holborn
London
EC1R 5BX

Magic Books by Post
29 Hill Avenue
Bedminster
Bristol
BS3 4SN

Louis Tannen, Inc.
6 West 32nd Street
4th Floor
N.Y., New York 10001
U.S.A.

Jeff Busby Magic, Inc.
The Barnard Building
612 Cedar Street
Wallace
Idaho 83873-2233
U.S.A.

If you have enjoyed reading and performing the tricks in this book, you will like its companion volume – *The Amazing Book of Magic* too. Magicians can perform magic with almost anything! *The Amazing Book of Magic* is a wonderful collection of tricks using ordinary objects that you will find around your home. In no time at all you will be performing tricks with coins, paper money, matchboxes, safety pins, string, cups, newspapers, silver paper, pencils etc. Each trick has been chosen to enable you, with just a little practice, to perform magic tricks anywhere, anytime!